CHRISTOP

A STUDY IN HUMAN PERSONALITY

BY

SIR OLIVER J. LODGE

AUTHOR OF "RAYMOND, OR LIFE AND DEATH," "THE SURVIVAL
OF MAN," "THE WAR AND AFTER," ETC.

NEW YORK
GEORGE H. DORAN COMPANY

CHRISTOPHER

CONTENTS

INTRODUCTION

PART I

PART II

MEMOIR, AUTOBIOGRAPHICAL FRAGMENT, AND REPRESENTATIVE LETTERS

ILLUSTRATIONS

CHRISTOPHER

INTRODUCTION

YOUTH AND THE WAR

"I with uncovered head
Salute the sacred dead,
Who went, and who return not.—Say not so!
'Tis not the grapes of Canaan that repay,
But the high faith that failed not by the way;
Virtue treads paths that end not in the grave;
No ban of endless night exiles the brave;
And to the saner mind
We rather seem the dead that stayed behind."
LOWELL, "Commemoration Ode."

IN this great massacre of youth, in which we are all, to the best of our ability, heavily engaged, having been driven thereto by the diabolical wickedness of a remorseless foe, what slaughter of heaven-sent genius must there inevitably be! Great and simple, high and low, all pass through the valley of the shadow, and many go the way to dusty death.

Of this great multitude the majority must be commonplace ordinary mortals, with potentialities undeveloped, and unlikely to be developed by the dull surroundings of ordinary routine.

A few there are who, though young, have already shown budding promise of distinction, and whose output is not negligible in quality, however deficient in quantity: these are lamented by the world; our loss in them is evident. But many more there must be whose latent capacity was only partially developed, who had had exceptional training, who might have risen to high position, who had laid a sure foundation for achievement, whose nerves and muscles, physical and mental, were in healthy condition, and who, by their intimates, were expected to do great things.

It is mainly of these unfledged songsters, these undeveloped athletes, these youths of blighted promise, that I write. Our loss in them, too, is serious, and the truncation of their own earth-life must be to them something of a calamity. They are born, they go through the troubles of infancy, they labour through strenuous years of preparation, love and care are showered upon them; and then, just in the flush of their ripening years, the blast comes which cuts them off untimely and returns them to that unknown world from whence in some mystic sense they came. All the ripening of experience, the discipline and judgment and forbearance which come with later years, they miss. And it is the best, alas! who go. Broadly this must be true.

Seen from our side, it looms large as a catastrophe, mitigated only by their heroism and self-sacrifice: to us, this unnatural selection, this survival of the unfittest, is deadly and depressing. What can we do but try to raise an altar to their memory, an altar before which many generations of posterity will bow in gratitude and homage! To this end poets and musicians and architects and artists of every kind will give of their best. A noble monument will be erected, stone by stone; and, buried in one of the stones, perhaps this volume may find a place.

But, however keenly we admire and rejoice in their achievements, we cannot help remembering how grievous and mechanical has been the slaughter. No longer can we sing of arms wielded by heroic men: armaments are now physical and chemical, the outcome of prostituted science. Complex machinery, against which human flesh is battered and helpless, flames for inflicting torment, poisonous gases in which no living creature can breathe—these diabolical engines are able to overcome and almost to annihilate heroism. The physiological collapse spoken of as shell-shock or war stress occurs among the bravest. War has become impossible and inhuman.

The undeveloped youth of humanity plunges into these horrors, and cannot hope to emerge scathless. The noble army of heroic youths, many of them heirs to privilege and comfort, willingly enter upon the toilsome and dangerous path. *Noblesse oblige.*

Hundreds and thousands of such youths in all ranks of life yield up their birthright of health and happiness, and either return maimed and disfigured or do not return at all. Some of those who are older or higher in rank may survive, it may be their duty to take precaution, but for the junior officer there is practically no hope of ultimate escape. They stand in the breach, they lead forlorn hopes, they obey the higher commands, and they fall—under the shower of shell and shrapnel they inevitably fall—sometimes having never seen a foe. Fall, I say; yes, fall to all appearance, but appearances are deceptive: they

> "fall to rise,
> are baffled to fight better,
> Sleep to wake."

Their task is far from ended, a completer existence is begun: they enter the ranks of higher service, their power of help is increased rather than diminished, and they still devote themselves to the cause for which they gave their lives.

Let it not be supposed that this noble army is helpless and supine; rather let us be sure that their performance of duty here was but the prelude to more extended service hereafter, that the welcome "Well done, good and faithful servant," will sound in their ears in due time, and that, as the outcome of their faithfulness in a few things, they will be entrusted with higher power, greater opportunity for achievement, a fuller measure of self-realisation, than would have been possible to them here and now. It is by their perfect willingness for service, and, if need be, for sacrifice, that they are enabled, in some real sense, to enter into the joy of their Lord.

For them all is gain; and even for us the gain will ultimately outweigh the loss. For we have not really lost them; they feel themselves to be nearer to us than before; death is no estrangement, it has been felt by

many as a kind of reunion. Body separates: spirit
unites.   These are statements based on evidence,
though the evidence must be sought elsewhere; what
is said here is the expression of a conviction which has
come to many.   And one thing more we know: sacrifice is the necessary prelude to the attainment of any
high aim.

The conflict in which we are engaged is not waged
by mechanical force alone, it is a knightly enterprise
of eager spirits and indomitable hopes.   In this struggle against principalities and powers and spiritual
wickedness in high places, we are not alone.   Our part
must be done, but it is shared in and assisted by agen-
cies higher than ourselves.   The aim towards which
all are striving is to liberate man from bondage to
material necessities, to revive opportunities for mental
and moral progress, to promote the peace-ensuring fed-
eration of civilised humanity, and to take a further step
toward the spiritual regeneration of mankind.

Why pick out for special remembrance one rather
than another of the glorious company of those who
have sacrificed themselves in this high cause?   Each
has done his duty, each is one of a type; but we can
best testify where we have known, and the more
closely we can represent the type the more valuable
will be our testimony.   With one such type—the
engineering practical type—I have in another book
already dealt.   I now essay the presentation of the
scholarly, the more artistic type, the undeveloped man
of letters or of statesmanship, the youth of intelligent

and cultivated emotion. Both types are full of humanity, full of promise, they sympathise with and understand each other, but their aptitudes lie in different directions, and we cannot tell how or along what lines their nascent genius would have led them, had they continued to live here.

Each may stand for a multitude, and I trust that many parents will realise, in one or other of those commemorated, a sufficient picture of what their own son was like, and will feel that in endeavouring to commemorate a few we are really commemorating a large and increasing number.

Now, in depicting a life cut off before its prime, the period of childhood must loom large. It is a period necessarily without achievement, but one which may be of singular interest and promise. It is a period, as I think, insufficiently attended to in many ranks of life, a period which seems short to adults, but which is very long to those who are passing through it, a period of which vastly more might by proper arrangement be made. One reason why the opportunities of this time of rapid growth are largely wasted, is our own adult stupidity, lack of imagination, and stress of other occupations. Another and more general cause of wholesale neglect is the nation's purblind economy, its emphasis on wage-earning, its failure to realise that the production of commodities at the expense of manhood and womanhood is devastating. But though multitudes have their youth spoiled and frustrated by a grievously sordid or depressing environment, some few, in happy homes and under wise guidance, are able to rise to the height of our common humanity so far as their years allow.

One undoubtedly who possessed such advantages is the subject of this memoir. And yet I see no reason to suppose that his native capacity was exceptional, unless it was exceptional in power of feeling and sympathy. Many a youth must be born with general ability equal to or exceeding his, some of them lower in social grade; and, if there were more real equality of opportunity, many of these might become of conspicuous service to the State. Every peer seems expected to be a statesman, or to be able at least to enter the diplomatic or some other form of service needing brains and character; and a large proportion of the well-born, whether as Governors of colonies or otherwise, show themselves more or less fit for high administrative office. It can hardly be because they are exceptionally gifted. Their success seems to show that the average of natural ability is fairly high, and that only nurture and opportunity are needed to bring out some capacity latent in every son of man.

But how little of this development do we attempt! It is lamentable to think that among the rank and file there must be a few whose potential genius is lost to the world, being warped and degraded by the stupidity and ignorance of adults or by short-sighted corporate greed.

It may be said that if youths have real genius they

can rise; and certainly some opportunities are now provided. Every now and then a Faraday or a Watt or a Stephenson shows what can be done in spite of difficulties, or with the help of timely patrons, and exhibits the latent capacity of the poor in birth. Mr. Smiles's volumes are full of the hard-won successes of men of this type. But our social system demands from members of the proletariat not only innate genius but a character of extraordinary strength, if they are ever to overcome economic difficulties, to emerge from the dead level of mediocrity, secure for themselves the necessary leisure, and come to high fruition. Of the wastage we hear less, but it must be appalling. Slaughter in war is but another and more obvious form of slaughter; it attracts more attention, but, save in quantity, it need hardly be more repined than the less obtrusive moral and intellectual slaughter always going on in time of peace.

The severity of war losses is felt by all classes, but is more conspicuous when the foresight of parents and the inheritance from previous generations have rendered wholesome development possible and comparatively easy; for those long years of preparation might have been expected to yield some worthy result, some reward for all the labour and sacrifice which had gone to the preparing of the way.

In some cases the hallmark of real genius may have been set upon a youth; the as-yet-undeveloped but nascent personality may have already displayed itself to expectant eyes; but the era of achievement was not yet; the bud and the blossom had appeared, but not the flower or the fruit.

"Childhood is genius without capacity," says Frederic Myers. Youth may have access to subliminal depths, may experience moments of intuition, may even display trailings of celestial glories, but, save in here and there a prodigy, it has had no adequate opportunity for incarnating much of itself in matter, it has not the skill to overcome the difficulties of translation, it cannot bring the meaning out into the light of day. Hidden but intense feelings, joys and pains more vivid than our worn souls remember, powers and insight of a depth barely suspected, all these can be characteristic of children, and of youths too whose development has not been checked by untoward circumstance, and whose ancestry has been able to bestow on them for generations the blessings of high culture.

And it is only fair if we comparatively useless survivors, loiterers it may be on a stage whence we must soon depart, should seek to realise and to represent something of what the cloud of vanishing youth has felt, something of what amid happier surroundings it will continue to feel, something out of which may yet arise a period of keener and wiser and more beneficent activity for man.

SUPPLEMENT TO INTRODUCTION

1. A Message to the Bereaved

The following message has already been privately circulated by the Author to bereaved friends, and it may suitably find a place here:—

The amount of mourning and suffering throughout Europe at the present time is something terrible to contemplate. The loss to those who have gone over is not to be minimised: violent death while young is a serious calamity—a man-made tragedy with dire consequences—and lamentation is natural and inevitable. But it must be remembered that, from the point of view of the individuals who have gone over, there are many mitigating circumstances. They have done their duty; they have sacrificed a useful career here; they have given up all they possessed; and it will be requited to them. By such a death a burden of sin is lightened; some atonement is made. Good friends are waiting for them; their help can be utilised, and is much wanted, for their fellows who are coming over; and they themselves will continue in the joy of service.

They would like their friends here to recognise that, and not to mourn them unduly; above all, not to consider them as gone out of existence, as extinguished and no longer real. Sorrow at their departure is inevitable, but grief which is excessive causes them pain.

They did their work here, they will do it there; and in good time reunion may confidently be looked forward to. If the truth of these matters was only clearly and widely realised, the mourning would be not only more resigned but actually more hopeful. Death alone is not to man the greatest evil, and in some sort they are happy in the opportunity of their death. This ought to be recognised by those who survive, and we should not grieve unduly for those who have only gone on before us.

2. A Vision of M. Maurice Maeterlinck's

"We must tell ourselves that now, in each of our homes, both in our cities and in the countryside, both in the palace

tudes of value in themselves, but ill-fitted to cope with some of the coarser and rougher aspects of youthful life.

It is a fairly accepted fact that the organism retraces rapidly the history of its ancestry, galloping through some stages with surprising swiftness. This historical repetition is not embryonic alone, it extends into childhood, and the infant presumably passes more or less quickly through the era of savagery, sometimes so quickly as to be barely noticed, sometimes prolonged by circumstances or by ill training until it comes to repulsive fruition in the comparatively unrestrained license of the hobbledehoy.

A small residual element of the prehistoric man may conduce harmlessly to love of sport. It may in some cases even tend to strengthen a character. There may be room in humanity for both the savage type and the studious type; it is no part of my function to criticise the order of things. But I apprehend that during the rise of humanity the period of unrelieved savagery has been more and more reduced; something of its merits should be retained, but it is to be hoped that during future ages of progress the studious, the inquiring, and more civilised type will have gradually constructed for itself an environment less hostile than at present, and that ultimately it will combine with its own peculiar virtues the strength of character inseparable from real elevation, and will become dominant. Already it has attained this stage in individuals, and the idea of weakness is far removed from my conception of the influences under which Christopher was reared.

The education and the companionship which he received from his Father was a noteworthy feature of his younger life. They rejoiced together in home games, including chess, billiards, and piquet, and in more frolicsome exercises in which the mother took but little interest. It was with his Father also that he began Greek, and though at a later period the boy's fresher learning forged ahead of the Balliol man's more rusty recollection, they went through a play of Aristophanes together with occasional squeals of laughter. The relationship between Father and Son continued to be of a most affectionate and almost fraternal character, and the shock of ultimate separation was severe.

The boy became an enthusiastic devotee of the Classics, and for his age I gather from competent testimony the impression that his scholarship was by no means despicable. He was entered upon the roll of Trinity College, Cambridge, and would undoubtedly have done well in the Classical Tripos, and keenly enjoyed the inspiration of his environment.

One of the greatest wrenches which he felt on going into the Army was the uprooting of his cherished ambition to go to Cambridge, and the abandonment, at least for a time, of the anticipated enjoyment of rooms in the Great Court of Trinity, wherein, when he tried for his scholarship, he had passed a glorious week.

Concerning Christopher's love of Classics, it was

obviously genuine and vivid—I feel instinctively his kinship with Frederic Myers, he was a boy with whom that Scholar would have had much sympathy—but naturally concerning matters of scholarship it is not for me to express an opinion. I have therefore secured testimony from a more than competent man of letters who knew the boy intimately, and who, in response to the question whether Christopher would have ever made a Scholar, answered somewhat thus:—

"Yes, of the real type; he would have developed, not on the side of philological minutiæ, but on the side of feeling for the Classics. It was an element natural to him. Other men might have had more exact technical knowledge, but few could have had a more human, a more spiritual, apperception and feeling for classical literature. It was in the stage of promise rather than of achievement; he was too young for technical competitions, but the authentic touch was there."

Of the Mother it is difficult and yet necessary to speak. As a woman of energy and ability she has been absorbed in war work of many kinds, she is an active member of a War Pensions and other Committees, and many there are, both among officials and among rightful beneficiaries, who can testify that it is no nominal service which she renders. She is, moreover, closely connected with Welsh Nationalist activities, having been Chairman of the Arts and Crafts Section of the National Eisteddfod of 1918, at which, in recognition of her services, the Archdruid conferred upon her the Honorary Eisteddfodic Degree of Ovate; and in the

Gorsedd Circle she is known by the Welsh name of *Mam o Nedd* (a mother of Neath). She is also one of the twenty original members (of whom three were women) elected at the Welsh National Conference in May, 1918, to form an Executive Committee for the purpose of forwarding the movement in favour of Self-Government for Wales on Federal lines. In all ways she holds a position of importance in South Wales, especially in the district of which Neath is the centre.

Through these, and her previous labours in the cause of Woman's Suffrage with Mrs. Fawcett and others, she must have become known to prominent people, especially to those interested in causes specially associated with the enterprises of women, or those in which women have recently been able to take a leading part; and locally she is a centre of enlightenment and gracious sympathy to her friends and dependents. It is difficult therefore to write of one so comparatively well known and still active; but inasmuch as what follows is a study of the development of the personality of a Youth and inasmuch as to this development the personality of the mother has contributed more than any other single cause, I am bound to speak of her as a woman of exceptional ability and strength of character, as well as of a human being specially characterised by sympathy and depth of feeling; for on all that there can be no shadow of difference of opinion. Depth of feeling, indeed, and passion of service, are chief among her special characteristics, and these innate attributes have been cultivated and brought out by Motherhood to a remarkable degree.

Devotion to her children is exemplified in her more than in most mothers, and the whole of her powers have been pressed into the service. A busy life has not prevented her keen appreciation of literature and art and music; and in all such directions, and in all matters of taste and of humanity, her influence on her children and immediate surroundings must have been profound.

Nor was it by inculcation only that the child's emotional life was fostered. Depth of feeling is a native gift, not an acquired character, and there can be no doubt about its inheritance. The perception of beauty in the boy was keen, artistic taste was highly developed, and more than in most families were expressions of affection and of enjoyment in life customary; the home atmosphere was one of healthy occupation and joy.

Many a boy may feel for his home circle a deep affection, few are either able or willing to express their feelings; they are usually self-contained until some strenuous call awakens their manhood, and out of the shyness and shamefacedness of boyhood they acquire the man's power of saying what he feels, undeterred by the old hypercritical and artificially restricted atmosphere of school.

I have emphasised the influence of the Parents, as is only natural and right. But among the home influences the younger sister Daphne was a strangely powerful one too. This child, destined to an early death, must have had an exceptional character, full of undeveloped possibilities, and the permanent influence of her brief life on those who had to do with her can hardly be over-estimated; it extended beyond the range of relationship, as letters testify. Length of days is no measure of a personal influence, there is something in genius which transcends time; and from the testimony of those who knew the infant I judge that nothing less than genius will account for the impression she made.

A memoir of her was written by her Mother a short time after the bereavement, and a portion of that will be added to this chapter as an illustration of the strength of the feelings which went to the making of the boy. The complete memoir has a beauty of its own; it was written under the immediate stress of heavy sorrow, and appears to me a human document of permanent value. It is only in a spirit of self-sacrifice that this and other private records are allowed to reach beyond the circle of close personal friends, but it is in epochs of stress that the emotional life is truly awakened, these epochs are of special though sacred value, and unless I am allowed to exhibit something of the depth of feeling which dominated the situation I cannot make the picture complete.

I know that a memoir about so young a child is exceptional. I have abbreviated it where I thought that abbreviation would not injure it, though I am not sure that abbreviation is an advantage. I regret that some of its poignant concluding portion has had to be omitted, but I make no apology for reproducing the

of July, 1908. No one could have thought of her as a baby; the first blossoms of the crown of childhood were already set about her brow before she was hid from my eyes, and it is as a child that I see her. . . .

In the words of the old game, Daphne reminds me of the following:

In flower	A hare-bell.
In tree	A willow in spring.
In sound	The lark's song.
In food	Fresh-drawn milk.
In melody	Old English airs.
In colour	A clear bright blue.
In scent	A primrose.

At Easter I went to Wales with Christopher, who had had whooping-cough at school, leaving Daphne in my mother's care. When we returned she and Nurse went up to 156, Sloane Street, so that Christopher and she might not meet. His quarantine was over, but we wished to run no risks. He was only in London about three days, and one morning called me excitedly to say The Darling was on the pavement opposite. Down we both ran, and in the open air brother and sister gazed at each other. They had not met since the end of January, and they were never to meet again here. Christopher loved her very dearly, and was proud of her. She was the cause of his first fight at school, some boy having named her in a teasing manner. . . .

Then comes the last earthly chapter of my dear child's story.

I had been out early that morning (Thursday, July 16th), and coming in about 11 o'clock I met her in the hall. She was in her pram, sitting up. The day was gusty, with now and then a slight drizzle of cold rain. Nurse said she would not take her far. It was the last day my darling child would ever sit in her pram or go out into the fresh air of this world—now all the fresh air of heaven is hers. Later in the day she became rather peevish, which was quite unlike her. I sent for the doctor, and by five o'clock he was there. A warm bath was ordered, and bed and quiet. There were no definite symptoms. She had a restless but not bad night. . . ,

[A portion dealing with the events of the three subsequent days is omitted.]

. . . . I kept the night-light burning, which gave a clear light. It made shadows on the ceiling; I can see them now. Not wishing to make a chair crack, I sat down on the floor beside the cot. From time to time I lifted myself up, and could see The Darling lying quiet. How I thanked God for the sleep; she had not had a moment's natural sleep for twenty-four hours. The wind must have been coming from the east, for I could hear Big Ben chiming the quarters, and then booming 3 o'clock. The silence of the night was unbroken; through the curtains I saw the first faint streak of dawn. Suddenly I noticed a change in The Darling's breathing. . . .

[A description of the child's peaceful passing is omitted.]

Day had broken, the moon still showed above the barracks roof, there was not a sound anywhere save of awakening birds. In that peaceful hour I was alone with my child's free spirit, blessing her and giving God thanks for her, and knowing the nothingness of what is called Death—such a word for the birth of the soul into perfect freedom and everlasting life! . . .

. . . . The Sun of Life had risen upon her and called her from our world of shadows. . . .

About 10 o'clock Canon Henson,[1] to whom I had written, came to us. We spoke, he and I alone together first—spoke of The Darling and of the future joy for us and the present joy for her. . . . Afterwards we all went into the nursery with him. The little sleeping form showed peaceful in the diffused light. He stood beside the cot, making the sign of the Cross, and saying, "Requiescat in Pace Christianum." Then he said, "Now we will say prayers." He gave thanks—the first note was that; he gave thanks for The Darling and all her pleasant ways and the joy she had brought, and thanks for the joy which she had reached. And he prayed that we might be helped and comforted "in this dark hour," and he commended The Darling's dear spirit to the love that called her into

[1] Now Bishop of Hereford.

being, and blessed her—to whom all blessings had come. It was the only religious note in all our Darling's going; and just such as we would have wished and felt appropriate. My mother, who heard the Church Service at Highgate, felt it almost grotesquely unreal, seeing that nothing of The Darling was contained in the little casket over which the Church seemed to be saying words implying a confusion of her identity with the mindless dust—the only real things there being poor Teddy Bear and White Bunny; real in the sense of being symbols of what loving hearts have fashioned for baby fingers from the times of the Egyptians, where tiny toys are found in tombs—and will continue to fashion down to the days when children of earth are no more. . . .

Of how I loved and love her I have not tried to speak; nor of my own sorrow: there is sorrow too deep for words, too absolute for healing tears. . . . I will end with these words, written to us by Canon Henson on the day our Darling rose to the life immortal: "I am grateful to you for letting me look on that lovely child—the sacrament of how fair a spirit, the cradle of how gracious a character. Perishable as the flower which rests on it, and yet having borne its witness, and fulfilled its task. The Life it brought and revealed to you endures and moves on to the full utterance of itself in His Presence, Who is the Life Everlasting; and you have its memory, and the hope of its restoration. May God bless you in the great sorrow of its absence, as He has blessed you in the great joy of its presence!"

CHAPTER II

SCHOOL DISCIPLINE

"What inconsistencies, what absurdities underlie the assumption that evolution means nothing more than the survival of animals fittest to conquer enemies and to overrun the earth. On that bare hypothesis the genus *homo* is impossible to explain. No one really attempts to explain him except on the tacit supposition that Nature somehow tended to evolve intelligence—somehow needed to evolve joy; was not satisfied with such an earth-overrunner as the rabbit, or such an invincible conqueror as the influenza microbe. But *how much* intelligence, *what* kind of joy Nature aimed at—is this to be left to be settled by the instinct of *l'homme sensuel moyen?* or ought we not rather to ask of the best specimens of our race what it is that they live for?—whether they labour for the meat that perisheth, or for Love and Wisdom? To more and more among mankind the need of food is supplied with as little conscious effort as the need of air; yet these are often the very men through whom evolution is going on most unmistakably— who are becoming the typical figures of the swiftly changing race."

F. W. H. MYERS, "Human Personality," chap. iii.

THE so-called Public Schools of England are collectively a great, a really magnificent institution; with splendid buildings, hallowed associations, and ancient traditions; full-filled they are with ancestral emotion, with all the accumulated feeling of generations of the well-born and well-to-do.

"Here," said Mr. Mackail, speaking of Eton, "one

feels, as perhaps nowhere else, the majestic continuity of the national life."

As for the staffing of these great schools, many of the headmasters are already half-way to the Bench of Bishops and the House of Lords; while the house masters, let us hope—it is always permissible though sometimes extravagant to hope—are adequately remunerated for their vitally important function, are as enthusiastic as any preparatory-school master about proper and sufficient semi-parental care of boys, both moral and material, at a critical and growing age; are without temptation to any kind of profiteering, and have sufficient wisdom to draw the difficult line between pampering on the one hand and neglect on the other. It must be admitted, however, that theirs is a most difficult and strenuous task, and that failure to rise to the heights of opportunity is bound to be frequent. Moreover, in the past at least, the luxury of home life has been too often an adverse influence. Yet this war, like every other, has demonstrated how splendid, in reality, is the raw material on which they have to work; though, hampered apparently by a curious kind of group-selfconsciousness, that material is apt to assume in self-defence a rather stupidly prosaic and hypercritical attitude to things in general, especially things of the emotions, and to affect a premature variety of cheap cynicism which is not easily overcome.

To the fostering care of these great institutions are entrusted the best-born and the otherwise privileged youths of England, and here they begin training for the work of life, preparation for taking the lead in industrial enterprises, and for ruling men in Dependencies throughout the British Empire. So much has been written in description and glorification of Public-School influence, in moulding character and determining destiny, that no more words are needed; nor need the multitude of such books be added to, even by a sentence, in order to emphasise merits which can be taken for granted. Had they not many virtues so many youths would not be sent there.

But in the midst of the praise, a critical voice is heard, and criticism is growing in intensity. Parents are anxious; questions are asked; replies are discordant or are difficult to obtain. Is everything really of the best, is it even as good as it might be? Is the discipline wisely conceived and properly carried out in these originally monastic institutions, or are boys of various ages left too much to their own devices? Do the weakest go to the wall? Are there not excesses, is not the boy-managed discipline too suddenly severe, the contrast with home and preparatory school too complete? Are the bodily exercises or "sports" overdone, giving rise to subsequent heart-strain and other troubles? [1] Is the feeding wholesome and adequate, or must it be supplemented from home?

[1] I only speak feelingly of long school runs, in which smaller boys are swished to over-exertion and fainting by bigger ones who are actuated by sheer ignorance and stupidity. At a school in Yorkshire this system of preposterously long competitive runs was in vogue, perhaps still is; and I have had occasion, not in my own person but in my own family, to curse it and its sequelæ.

Many such questions are asked, and I do not presume to answer them: they have to be answered differently, it may be supposed, at different schools, and even at different periods in the same school.

All I have to say, or to suggest, concerning school life is absolutely general; it has no reference to any one school in particular. Special and intimate knowledge would be required for that. But there are certain general characteristics which without controversy can be admitted—characteristics some of which are upheld by high authority as sound and wholesome and beneficent. Let us consider one well-worn argument in their favour.

The discipline and hardship of school are said to prepare a boy for the discipline and hardship of later life. The note struck is preparation. So far, good. Preparation for life is eminently desirable; and the particular preparation afforded by school life appears to be considered a kind of inoculation. For in like manner it may be said that inoculation prepares one to resist the ravages of specific disease when that is encountered in the future.

Inoculation is admittedly never a pleasant process, though authority says that it is necessary. Let us accept that. But we do not select the most virulent form of microbe for inoculation purposes, we do not apply the disease in its severest form to prepare against milder attacks in the future. Yet, according to the testimony of many, the hardship and discipline of school during say the first year, and even during subsequent years for many boys, are harsher and more grievous than anything they can reasonably expect to encounter in later life. In later life if we make mistakes we are punished, it may be by a fine, it may be by seclusion, but we are not flogged, except for brutal crimes; nor are we beaten by a jury of our fellows, or by some individual stronger than ourselves, unless we have injured him in a quite exceptional way, in some way so serious that he is moved to take the law into his own hands. We are not placed helpless in the midst of a community whose members are of very varying degrees of size and strength, with traditional powers over body and sometimes soul, where tale-bearing is forbidden, and where we are removed from the curbing or protective agency of the police. No one expects to encounter troubles of this kind; and to inoculate against the risk of it seems carrying precaution rather far.

In later life when we run into danger we take other precautions. If we go among savages we carry weapons of precision; if we encounter civilised ruffians we appeal to the arm of the law; we protect ourselves against bodily ill-treatment in various ways, and our souls are our own.

But it will be said that at an earlier stage of life we are retracing an evolutionary period, that we all have to go through the savage phase, and that in this phase the rough discipline of school is salutary and not alien to our disposition. To some, I suppose, it does seem natural and right; but to those whose savage period is curtailed or galloped through, and who already at an early age have reached a higher stage of civilisation, the alien character of the mixed elements of school life becomes painfully apparent.

But it is not alone, it is not even mainly, the mere physical roughness and irresponsibility of seniors that I propose to criticise. These are painful, but some people can conscientiously maintain that they are salutary, that they are good for the small boy, and do not injure the big boy or develop any vein of cruelty in his disposition. At any rate, they do not seem to frustrate the main purpose for which schools exist. This purpose I conceive to be development of intellect and of character. Some call it "formation" of character, and put it first. If formation of character is possible by outside influences, then indeed those influences become supremely important; but character must be to a great extent inborn. It may be unfolded, or it may be withered, its development may be helped or hindered; but surely a school should develop character mainly through the intelligence. Awakening of the mind would seem to be a main necessity in any scholastic scheme. A system of training which depresses the mind and yet keeps it at mental tasks for several hours a day, until a feeling of nausea or study-nostalgia is created which lasts more or less through life, few would have the hardihood to support: they can only deny that any such state of things exists; and can take refuge in maintaining that assertion of this kind is an accusation and misrepresentation made by some enemy.

Well, such assertions are made and must be faced. I

wish to write tentatively, but I ask those who know the real facts, whatever they are, to consider why such accusations have ever been made. So far as I am able to judge of the matter, basing my view on information available to all, and seeking earnestly to avoid exaggeration, I feel bound to say something on the subject of school, as it not invariably but too often is; and with this apology as preface I begin.

To a sensitive boy the period of school is a strange admixture of good and evil, of pleasure and pain. With some the pain predominates over the pleasure, and it is difficult to deny the assertion that with a few the evil predominates over the good. A friend of boarding-school education can hardly contest the statement that it is, or has been, characterised by some features which may be called defects. Such are:—

> Discouragement of intellectual keenness.
> Suppression of natural emotional expression.
> Reduction of exuberant individuality to a common type.
> Submission to a dull tradition of stupid uniformity, where every action has to be guarded by deference to public opinion, on pain of punishment.

That these are characteristics of public schools, where boys of different ages are left to the tender mercies of each other, to the discipline of prefects, and subject to unwritten laws which are Draconian in their severity, can hardly be denied. That they are merits, few will have the hardihood to assert. And if they are not merits they are faults, out of which it is to be hoped that the wave of reality which has submerged us in the great war will have sufficient residual power to emancipate us before it has subsided.

Joy in rational study, eagerness to receive information—though perhaps not from books—desire to understand something of the nature of our surroundings and of the main interests of life, these are possessions surely natural to most children, though apparently not to all. But this kind of joy and eagerness is often killed in the growing youth: and for this catastrophe I feel bound to accuse, first the unwisdom, indeed the ignorance, of teachers, and next the more or less suffocating atmosphere of school. Desire for knowledge may in exceptional cases return with but little abatement during a College period or in later life, but during the priceless years of boyhood it must be hidden, it must be indulged secretly if at all; an atmosphere of apathy and magisterial cynicism too often succeeds in killing it.

Few teachers seem to cultivate desire for knowledge when it needs cultivation, though of course there are exceptions [1]; schools may have many merits—doubt-

---

[1] Much has been said, and much needs to be said, about lack of scientific training in the past, and about methods adopted for teaching science, in the present. I feel strongly that no person can be considered educated who grows up without some unspecialised information and clear outlook on the universe of matter, both animate and inanimate, of which he is a part. I also consider that it is easy to be too specific and technical in imparting this information to the average unscientific boy with no special aptitude for the subject; and that a course of unprofessional or humanistic science might with

less they have—but as a rule intellectual encouragement is not one of them.   If that is in any degree true
it would be difficult to frame a more serious indictment.

The lumbering crudeness of the average professional
schoolboy hides, and in normal life effectively conceals,
a multitude of virtues.   His professionally guarded
attitude, undemonstrative, reserved, incapable of intelligent expression, and yet with sensitive tentacles
shrinking at a touch from his fellows, is like the shell
of a crustacean, a protective covering which inevitably
hinders free development and which, in more favour-
able surroundings, ought not to be necessary.   This
protective crust can hardly be the result of any reasonable discipline, and in so far as it tends to cramp the
wholesome exercise of faculties it is noxious.   Nor is its
cramping influence over the higher faculties limited to
the school period.   It lasts into Sandhurst and other
establishments where men of good physique learn self-
government under strict but intermittent discipline,
and where warped high spirits are responsible for occasional outbursts of rowdiness or even ill-treatment.
The tendency too often is to regard a new-comer as
easy prey.   At Winchester, and doubtless in other
schools, an elder boy is, I believe, told off to help and
befriend a new-comer for a time, and in many ways
authority tries to stem the influence of meaningless tradition; but at some schools a new boy seldom experi-

advantage be devised.   But it is inappropriate to enter upon topics
like this in the present book.   I wrote an article in the *Fortnightly
Review* for August, 1918, on the subject.

ences the smallest chivalry or kindly help in his initial difficulties, and can easily be rendered miserable, while in the worst cases the thoughtless power of the stronger develops into an obscene brutality.

Not with such aid would one expect a Commonwealth to be saved. And yet here are our defenders and underneath the crust they are fine fellows all the time. Hence all these troubles are unnecessary. They thwart and spoil the incubation period. They dissipate energy. Many are the evils which come to fruition in times of peace, when the output of energy is greater than the demand for its exertion. Only a call is needed—a summons to danger and responsibility—for true manhood to assert itself. Expression then bursts its hard crust, human nature is once more free as in childhood, the hero at the front is once more at liberty, emancipated from the painful protective casing in which his personality was masked and even his family affection partially obscured.

Christopher left behind an unusually complete self-revelation, for among his papers was found a locked manuscript book, the contents of which had never been seen by anyone, not even by his mother, till after his death. Here he collected, for private edification, poems and passages which struck him as of permanent value; and, in addition to these, the book contains as its longest feature an autobiographical fragment written during the period of military training with the Welsh Guards at Tadworth Camp. This is reproduced in Chapter VI., and to my mind it serves to show

how unsuited he and his type are to the rough-and-tumble of an average public school as now constituted. But let it not be thought that the fault lay in the boy, that he was a milksop or unable to play the man. No such idea would have occurred to those who knew him; and fortunately I am able to cite clear evidence to the contrary, in the letters from officers at the front which are reproduced in a concluding chapter of this book. In all the realities and exigencies of strenuous life he made himself respected, he made himself beloved: respected by his colleagues, beloved by his men. The testimony from all ranks is strong, spontaneous, and clear.

The autobiographical fragment breaks off—perhaps fortunately—at the end of his experience of the Preparatory School. What he felt afterwards in his main school days can only be gathered between the lines of his letters home, for apparently he had not the heart to confess it even to his locked book. Those who have been through it know: though there is a glamour thrown over early days, when reviewed in later life, which masks much of the tedium, the bitter disappointment, the chilling frost of misunderstanding and lack of sympathy. Some indication of the lower activities of officers in training at Sandhurst are given in the letters of that period which follow: corresponding indications of the school period are harder to find. The natural exhilaration of boyhood, the desire to save his parents anxiety, the traditional feeling of loyalty, the danger of any information reaching the ears of authority, all combine to render a small boy at school helpless and secretive and inexpressive to a remarkable degree. But in Christopher's case, characterised by an unusually close bond of intellectual and moral sympathy between mother and son, a few facts were revealed, which though regarded as private ought not to be concealed if the representation of school life is not to be altogether one-sided and therefore misleading. The fact to be faced is that to him and to his type school life is not really happy. It is only made tolerable by a blunting of the nerves, a case-hardening of the intelligence, a yielding up of individuality, and a drifting with the crowd. Separation from home is one inevitable burden, most felt perhaps at the preparatory school, where pains and penalties of a more active character hardly exist. Home-sickness is bad enough, but in another sense the school-sickness of a later period is much worse. Those who have been through it will recognise some of their own reminiscences in the few more private letters which I think it well to include in order to make the representation complete. These sadder portions written by the boy at the age of seventeen must be allowed not unduly but sensibly to qualify the happier tenour of the main batch of letters reproduced in the "Winchester" chapter.

Loyalty to an institution of which they once formed part and in which they made some friends, must be made responsible for the would-be comforting assurance of elders that school life is necessarily happy.

Happy in some respects it is, as all exuberant youth is happy, but we need not blind ourselves to its deficiencies or fail to realise how much better and more stimulating it could be made. The sort of happiness achieved by the less civilised kind of boy—the average for whom up to the present the institutions would seem to have been more particularly devised—is dearly bought.

To these average specimens the rest are more or less sacrificed. They represent the type for which rules and regulations are planned, they represent the type to which accordingly it is less troublesome if every other kind of boy is made to conform.

The stupidity of the conventional atmosphere of schools in general is illustrated by the biographies of many—one might almost say of most—great men, at any rate of those who do not shine in the world of books. Sometimes it is a great naturalist who tells us that he "learnt next to nothing at school;" sometimes it is a traveller or engineer or man of science. How often one reads something like this: "At school his genius was not discovered, the masters considered him rather stupid;" or, "He must have developed late, for no suspicion of his future eminence appears to have been entertained by either his teachers or schoolfellows." I quote the following sentence from a biography of James Clerk Maxwell, one of the greatest mathematical physicists of all time, who died at the early age of 48—too little known even then by the stolid British public in general, though a household word on the more educated Continent of Europe, and more than a pioneer, a founder, of the highest developments in electro-optical and molecular science:—

"At school, he did not at first take a very high place, and his schoolfellows so much misunderstood the character of the reserved, dreamy boy, that they gave him the nickname of 'Dafty.' "[1]

The very business of a school is to deal with many varieties of young humanity, and its pride should be to recognise and develop nascent ability in whatever direction it begins to blossom; therefore a school system which has only one standard of judgment, and practically penalises by neglect or misunderstanding all who do not conform to that standard, inevitably writes itself down in terms akin to that in which the indignant Dogberry longed to have himself recorded.

The contrast between a school or a Sandhurst atmosphere on the one hand, and the tone of the letters received from Christopher when he emerged into the comparative freedom and adult sanity of Tadworth Camp and of the Trenches, is very marked. And yet what a condemnation it is that such a nature could feel less out of place and homeless even amid the hardships and horrors of war than he felt while at school! For these hardships were real, earnest, and inevitable—given the present state of humanity and the blasphemy of a super-ambitious enslaving nation which had to be curbed by force; but the other troubles were gratuitous, unseemly, petty and un-

[1] Schuster and Shipley, "Britain's Heritage of Science."

worthy: they represented the forcible return of a civilised being to savagery. And even that is unfair, for savages at their best are only childishly human and natural, and with them we may have and may show a fellow feeling; but with the arbitrary conventions and brutal traditions of an irresponsible assemblage of privileged ignoramuses there can and ought to be no alliance. Submission is necessary, for they have force on their side, but it is always ignominious; for it is not genuine human nature that is encountered, but various forms of what can only be stigmatised as vice. I mean nothing technical by this word—though of that, too, something might be said—but I mean any behaviour which runs counter to what is natural, any conduct based on rules which are formal, constricted, empty, and profane, including every kind of evil conduct which is not even justified or partially excused by normal and natural temptation.

Even games can be spoiled by compulsoriness and semi-professionalism. Playing cricket for his platoon at a later stage was enjoyable, and was entered into with zest; it was a real relaxation and a friendly game, accompanied by pleasure and pride in the comparative prowess natural to a Public-School boy. But drudging at games amid the harshness of school discipline, as if they were an end in themselves and alone worthy of strenuous exertion, was no true relaxation, and little better than another form of toil.

Unless schools are already perfect, improvement must be possible, and when improvement is admitted it becomes only a question of degree. There are some who feel that the scope open to improvement is both wide and deep. And, in spite of admiration for many excellent qualities, it seems to me that to a larger extent than is commonly admitted, they are right.

CHAPTER III

MILITARY PREPARATION

"We know not in what directions—directions how definitely pre-determined—even physical organisms can vary from the common type. We know not what amount of energy any given plant or animal can absorb and incorporate from earth and air and sun. Still less can we predict or limit the possible variations of the soul, the fulness which it may receive from the World-Soul, its possible heritage of grace and truth. But in genius we can watch at each stage the processes of this celestial nurture. We can imagine the outlook of joyous trustfulness; we can almost seem, with Wordsworth, to remember the child's soul entering into the Kingdom of Heaven. Childhood is genius without capacity; it makes for most of us our best memory of inspiration, and our truest outlook upon the real, which is the ideal, world."

MYERS, "Human Personality," chap. iii.

WITH such parentage and surroundings the boy is launched upon the world, type of many another product of cultivated English homes. Slowly the boy develops from the child, and manhood gradually dawns upon the boy. What his career would have been in times of peace, with his quiet tastes, his affectionate disposition, his love of everything connected with Wales and the Welsh people, his passionate devotion to his home, and the opportunities which, in the course of nature, he would have possessed of taking his rightful place as heir to a property situated in an industrial district where labour problems are especially acute, and where already he was becoming well known and popular—of all this nothing can now be said.

Every scheme was shattered by the outbreak of War and by the attainment of an age when military service became possible.

Without enthusiasm, indeed with constitutional repugnance to the illogical gruesomeness of war, in full knowledge of the degradation which had fallen upon so-called civilised warfare, he and his kind entered upon the training necessary to fit them for military service, and in his case to enable him to attain the coveted honour of becoming an Officer in the Welsh Guards. And it must be said that he succeeded brilliantly.

Considering the extremely short time which he had at the actual Front, for within a month from going abroad he met his death, the spontaneous testimony to his disposition and capabilities, his admirable behaviour under stress, and his high powers as a soldier— such concurrent testimony both from officers and men is amazing.

Courage and high bearing are innate qualities in a British gentleman, truly, but it is good to know that, having undertaken an irksome task, he threw himself into it with vigour and characteristic thoroughness, and succeeded in winning golden opinions from those well qualified to judge.

The hardships of a winter campaign and of the long

fatigue of the trenches he was spared,—in this more fortunate than many of his comrades. One after another of those who went out with him have likewise now succumbed, and the roll of glory inexorably grows.

Among so many heroic lads, why pick out one for special mention? I have a reason; and the reason in the next chapter will be clear.

The belief in continuity of existence, in survival of the spirit of man beyond bodily death, was as keen and vivid and as free from doubt or hesitation in his family as in any that I have known. The death of his sister Daphne, in some indirect way, had contributed to this in no small measure; and the result of this strong belief, or, as it seemed, knowledge, was extraordinarily wholesome. It led to an agreement between Mother and Son providing for all contingencies, it bore fruit in an attitude of clear-eyed faith and unrepining acquiescence in whatever happened, a thoroughness of acquiescence in the inevitable, which, though it may not be unique, is practically without similar example in my knowledge.

It is in the earnest hope that agreements of this kind, based on faith of equal strength, will become commoner—agreements which shall mitigate the severity of the pain which so many must still undergo in the near future,—it is largely in the hope that the discovery here made, of how to meet impending fate and insure against the repercussion of bodily injury on the mind and soul, may be helpful to others, that this book is written.

In a previous volume I dealt, as impersonally as possible, with a family where posthumous comfort was obtained, and undoubted communication received, across the thin veil of separation; but many there are who, perhaps wisely, decline to seek or are unable to gain comfort in this way. "Many are the thyrsus-bearers, few are the mystics." For these, and perhaps for all, I am now permitted to show another and perhaps more excellent way.

Both methods are sensible and right and well-founded; but temperaments differ, opportunities do not come equally to all. Yet all alike suffer in this terrible eruption of mad violence; all of every class must give of their heart's blood to stem the onset of the beast; and it surely behoves us, to whom after much study insight has been given, to supply such help, such encouragement, such strengthening of the mental and moral sinews, as shall enable others to meet the worst in a spirit of calm endurance,—nay rather, to meet it in a triumphant spirit of steadfast faith and hope and love.

CHAPTER IV

THE COMPACT

"If the belief in a life to come should ever regain as firm possession of men's mind as of old, that belief will surely be held in a nobler fashion. That life will be conceived, not as a devotional exercise nor as a passive felicity, but as the prolongation of all generous energies, and the unison of all high desires."

MYERS, "Modern Essays," viii., p. 310.

"Not, then, with tears and lamentations should we think of the blessed dead. Rather we should rejoice with them in their enfranchisement, and know that they are still minded to keep us as sharers in their joy. It is they, not we, who are working now; they are more ready to hear than we to pray; they guide us as with a cloudy pillar, but it is kindling into steadfast fire.

"Nay, it may be that our response, our devotion, is a needful element in their ascending joy; and God may have provided some better thing for us, that they without us should not be made perfect; *ut non sine nobis consummarentur.*"

MYERS, "Human Personality," chap. x.

IT is naturally to be expected that a family connected by marriage with F. W. H. Myers, even though they had come but little into contact with that vehement personality, should have heard of his dominating interest, and absorbed some of his ideas concerning survival and the nature of a future life. Yet not till after the challenging, and to the Mother devastating, event of the death of Daphne did the subject force itself conspicuously on their conscious attention; and when it did, the channels through which enlightenment came were not the recognised commonplaces of religion or the traditional beliefs of any sect, but were derived from the inspiration of poets and men of letters, and from some of the facts on which Myers himself had based his own philosophic conceptions: though it is probable that the facts were but partially known, and the conceptions perhaps imperfectly apprehended.

The result, however, was a homely and practical and, so to speak, secular outlook on the continuity of existence, treating after-life not in an awe-stricken scared manner, but with full recognition of duties to be done, affection to be felt, and life to be lived; treating it, in fact, very much as if the lost ones were only separated by some not altogether impenetrable veil, or as if they had emigrated to another land, a land full of interest and beauty, though out of reach of the ordinary opportunities for domestic intercourse.

Wherever such belief prevails, it is only natural that every means of continuing the unbroken family feeling should be employed. Relics, reminiscences, anniversaries, everything which reminded the family of its dead member, would be kept in the forefront of attention; and the silent influence, the still half-realised presence of the loved one, would be felt as a stimulus and an assistance in daily life. The first shock of debilitating pain over, a healthy reaction would begin; and the determination would be made to live life worthily, and to serve strenuously, until the time came for corporate re-union.

In this faith I doubt not the boy Christopher was reared. And it is noteworthy that the paralysing shock of Daphne's death, felt to an almost overpowering extent by the mother, indirectly led her to take precautions against any repetition of so shattering a blow: so that nine years later, when the boy was ready to go to the Front and enter the zone of danger from which escape was obviously precarious, a solemn compact was entered into between mother and son, the effect of which proved to be strengthening and comforting and helpful on both sides to an extraordinary degree. And its influence endured long after the first excitement had subsided, and endures in unabated strength to this day.

This compact it is a chief part of my duty to emphasise and to commend to others; for I have been impressed with its unique value, and I had not heard before of any similar compact so clearly made and so thoroughly carried out.

Compacts made between relatives expecting to be separated by death, that, if possible, they would endeavour to communicate and send some loving greeting from the other side of the grave, or would otherwise give some proof of their continued existence—compacts such as these are common. I say nothing against them, they are natural enough, but they are most appropriate when made between people torn with the agony of doubt, eager to be convinced, seeking for a sign. There is no sense of security, no assured repose, about a compact of that kind; it breathes of uncertainty, almost of hopelessness, it is like the longing for a miracle in order that faith may be strengthened; it is entirely justifiable, but in most cases it is a sign of feeble faith, at least on one side.

Not of such nature was the compact that I now speak of. It was the outcome of clear and vigorous certainty, based largely upon testimony no doubt, but upon intuition too. The fact of survival was admitted; the possibility of some kind of communication was assumed; the shock of separation was faced; but no demand was made, on either side, for evidence of continued existence or surviving affection.

Everything of that kind was taken for granted. Given that the departed remained himself, a sudden extinction of love was inconceivable. No sign of survival was needed; the certainty of continued existence was already assured.

Hence what was needed was not preoccupation with things or people left behind, not groping after what had ceased to be possible—the old familiar handclasp, the old loving embrace, the welcoming bodily presence —not these, but a clear perception that a new life was being entered on, new surroundings to be understood, old friends to be welcomed in a new guise, a multitude of interesting and absorbing things confronting the new comer. Among these he would be moving as a novice, and it was hoped that he might move secure and unperturbed, eager and interested, unperplexed

and unsurprised. To this initial stage it was desirable
that he should give himself wholly, not restrained or
hampered by anxiety for the grief, still less by the unnerving doubts, of those left behind. Their sorrow,
for the time, he might safely ignore, if only he could
be sure that they would sympathise with and understand his attitude, would themselves be endeavouring
to take up the broken fragments of their own life, and
without repining, with no undue mourning, would un-
dertake or continue the tasks which lay before them,
and, like him, give to those tasks their undivided attention.

The aim was that each might feel secure of the
other,—secure that temporary absorption did not signify forgetfulness, secure that no misunderstanding
would arise or distrust be caused by absence of any
sense of communion for a time.

A sense of communion might well come hereafter,
after an interval perhaps not long; but meanwhile it
was determined that whatever opportunities for communication might in due time follow, they need not
be hurried, that nothing need interfere with the happy
and peaceful readjustment of existence to the new
and for a time strange condition. Such was the compact, and it was the clear outcome of mutual love and
faith.

Some people imagine that belief in survival of an
assured kind will lead people to neglect their mundane
duties and be always asking for messages and evidence;

but they are mistaken. Excessive demands of this kind are a sign of weak faith.

For scientific purposes evidence is necessary, and may be legitimately sought. People who cannot believe, and who grope after some hope of continued existence, require tests and evidence too. All this is right and human enough. In moderation it is helpful and reasonable for all. But once let the fact of survival be fully and finally established, on scientific not on superstitious grounds, once let the general manner of it be understood, its nature and laws duly recognised, and a far more peaceful attitude will be taken towards death and towards the departed.

That memory survives will be known, that affection is permanent will not be doubted. These will be among the facts apprehended by humanity in general, like the roundness of the earth.

And once this knowledge is universal and secure, then, though occasional communion will still be desired, as is only natural, only those who felt half doubtful of real affection here will anxiously seek for evidence that in each individual instance the love of the departed was really strong enough to survive the shock of death and to continue amid the manifold interests of another state of being.

In order to show how different from this was the attitude of Mother and Son here commended, I have obtained permission to copy some extracts from private letters and records which will in some measure speak for themselves.

66 CHRISTOPHER

They prove how immediately the compact took effect. Further testimony can be adduced that the effect was not an evanescent excitement, to give way to subsequent depression, but that it burned with a clear and steady flame, and so continues to this day.

Concerning the Compact

Copy of a letter written by Christopher's Mother to his immediate relations on September 10th, 1917, four days after hearing of his having fallen in action.

Cadoxton, September 10th, 1917.
8:30 a.m. Monday.

I want you all to know just exactly what *is* about what has happened.

On August 3rd, just one month before Cruff's[1] rising, he was here. We had our first long talk together alone since both had known of his going abroad. We sat—holding each other's hands, and not without tears. We knew what it was to both of us, and we wanted to say certain things between us.

After speaking of the perfect companionship which was always ours, but had flowered into such beauty as the boy emerged towards manhood, we spoke of the future, and we provided definitely and fully *for each of us* what we should each do, aim at, and feel, under certain eventualities.

These were—that he should be wounded, or missing, or taken prisoner, or killed in action.

[1] The abbreviation "Cruff" was used only in writing.

We have only to meet this last, and I want you all to know what we arranged, and therefore what *is*.

We decided that sudden death must be a shock, and that if Cruff found himself suddenly "over there" he was to *expect* to be conscious of Daphne and Fred [1]— and if they were not there he was to inquire for them at once. He was then to give his whole mind to the business in hand—*i.e.* to getting his bearings in the new environment, and was to keep before his mind that I was all right, that I knew he was all right and entirely himself and unchanged, and that I was steadying him and helping him telepathically.

And for me it was settled between us that I should hold to what we both knew as truth—that though the old companionship of bodily life was broken the deeper intimacy was already begun. My part was to know for him what he would wish to say to me, and to feel *all* the cheerful jolly nearness of him and me unchanged, to refuse grief as a disturbing element—and to make Cadoxton a happy-hunting ground for him as we had always agreed it was for The Darling.

We agreed that Fred's presence over there made any strangeness impossible, and that we could never, either Christopher or I, feel anything *past* between us. You see neither he nor I ever thought of Death as more than a doorway admitting to fuller and freer life.

When I went to the telephone on Thursday night and took the message from the War Office, I was alone for five minutes, and in that time I slipped my hand firmly into his and *began my part*, as he, un-known to me, had begun his part a few days earlier.

[1] F. W. H. Myers.

I had been terribly anxious before. I knew he was in the trenches; all that dropped away. One of the eventualities we had provided for had come, and it was so unutterably blessed to think we were *together* in a mutual experience we had discussed and provided for.

If I had known he had to give his life in war—which was utterly foreign to his type of mind and character—I should have chosen for him myself just such a death, and on his first going into action. It was a sudden sleep and a sudden awakening—nothing to forget. I go through these days and the long, long nights, just holding his hands—as if he were coming out of an anæsthetic, and as if my dear familiar face, just there, without speech, was what he needed. We both of us know the truth, and he is, I believe, deeply happy. He always looked to me for love and strength, and I shall not fail him now.

This is not to say that there isn't a side of me which is bleeding—but it is not the deeper side; and he and I, we will accept that side too as inevitable, seeing beneath it what is true to the depths of both of us.

I want everyone to know this and to help him and me by confirming us in our resolutions.

DAPHNE'S MOTHER.[1]

To this main contemporary statement about the compact, a few further extracts may be appended, all taken from letters to other members of the family. The first of them describes what the home circle did immediately after they had heard the news: which they

---

[1] This is a signature frequently used by Christopher's mother when writing to intimate friends.

received through a War Office telegram, transmitted from Cardiff Post Office by telephone at 8.15 p.m. on September 6th, 1917, three days after the event.

Extract from a letter written by Christopher's Mother on September 7th, 1917, *the day after she heard of his death.*

. . . we went into the drawing-room and sat—as if listening—trying to understand. My whole desire is not to fail Cruff now: he always looked to me for love and strength, the one thought in his mind if he was not killed instantaneously must have been me—and C. C. T. During those days from the Sunday to last night I didn't know, and was very anxious and depressed; now I know, and shall never be anxious about him again, and what I am doing is to try and strengthen and *steady him* in the new surroundings. It is a shock being killed like that. He has . . . [a friend] and Fred—towers of strength—Daphne, Papa, and many comrades, Atkins and others. If he was killed suddenly it may have been some little time before he could be made to understand that he was what we call "dead." That is what makes me sit here struggling to let him find here in his home nothing but love and understanding of what has happened to him. He is to me as if just out of a severe operation—my steady hand in his is what he needs now, for he loved me much . . . I have no agonies of mind as to where his dear young body lies—it has served his purpose and he has outgrown the need of it; my deepest self knows only this—that he is utterly safe for ever, utterly unchanged, *undiminished*, his own bright, happy self. He will have the same capacity for making friends, he will soon get his bearings there, and whether he does it happily and easily, depends on what telepathic impression he gets from us—but especially from me. He can't speak to us—anyhow not yet—we have got to know in our minds, *for him*, what he is wanting to say.

Extract from another letter, of date September 23rd, 1917.

. . . I feel all you do, and wrestle against it because I am certain that if anything could unsettle him over there it would be the feeling that I was failing him. It is *we* who have to bear the burden, and *he* who reaps complete unchanging well-being.

"Is any burden sore when one's beloved go free?
Come pain and woe to me—my well-beloved goes free."

. . . Don't you find comfort in the thought that it can't be very long before you see him again—and then without *possibility* of any more partings? Life was always tearing him from me—school, Sandhurst, the war; when I see him face to face again all *that* will have ceased—once found I shall never be away from him again. It can't be so very long for any of us. (Set against the background of Eternity, *how short! !*) . . .

The same feelings and the same absence of prostrating grief or unreasoning and uncontrolled emotion have continued to this day—a victory won by the steadfast following of a high resolve.

In the light of this assured conviction and unselfish preparation and determined realisation of fact, how impious and distrustful appears the attitude of those who, dominated by mediæval or ante-mediæval priest-craft, seek anxiously to know the fate of their departed, torment themselves with hopes and fears, question whether they are "saved," try to pray them out of purgatory or else to suppress all mention of them in their prayers, and endeavour (often fruitlessly) to convince themselves that eternal fate is settled at once and for ever, beyond possibility of progress or recovery, at the instant of death!

Few people now go to this extreme length; though the amount of torment that has been caused by such beliefs in the past can hardly be exaggerated, and all this gratuitous pain must be debited to the account of those who promulgated and sustained so senseless a creed.

But many there are still who have anxious doubts and fears, who cannot accept the simple naturalness of a passing over into the unseen—*i.e.* into the super-sensuous where our earth-derived sense-organs are help-less—who fail to realise that we remain just ourselves, without sudden access of knowledge and without loss of such human faculties as are serviceable amid the new surroundings; surroundings after all, it may be, not so very different, at first, from those of earth.[1]   In

---

[1] If a working hypothesis which commends itself to me may be here obtruded, I should say that the change appears to be a liberation from matter, accompanied by a retention of our etherial connection; not so much the sudden acquisition of something, but the

no strange land do we find ourselves, if we have been reasonably prepared; and the shock of death will be greatly mitigated, to the survivor as well as to the departed, when more people are able to make a compact akin to the one here set forth and heartily commended.   I know of no better form of compact; free from superstition, void of anxiety, emancipated from over-specific or sectarian belief; full only of faith in cosmic wisdom and beneficence, anxious only that the lost one shall be worthy of his promotion, shall make full use of his advantages, and shall settle down as quickly and easily as possible to the enjoyment of his recovered friends and higher opportunities for progress.

For it is progress, not happiness, that should be most earnestly desired.   Happiness comes when not directly sought after; it should be among the things that are "added unto" those who, in any state of existence, seek to do their duty.

And of the innumerable boys who have gone to the front and entered the repulsive complication of modern war, with no taste for it whatever but solely from a sense of duty, how great must be the happiness that necessarily follows so sublime a sacrifice!

No survivor should doubt for a moment the destiny in store for such as these.   Not all of equal standard, truly; not all have had equal opportunities, every

retention of something which we already possess, though here and now its possession is only known to us by inference from indistinct phenomena—by, as it were, *larval* indications.

grade may be represented; social conditions have been hard on some, personal weakness has enfeebled others, but there is a place or condition suited to every grade, and into the state suited to him, each automatically and naturally enters; retaining his earth-grown character, for better for worse, but meeting a host of kindly helpers who will set him on his feet and turn his face in the right direction—the direction which on earth the higher part of himself, had it not been for the weakness of the flesh, would have desired to choose.

Distinct from the large group of people influenced by theological prejudice and superstitious uncertainties, there is another group who find it necessary to contend against the painful ignorance of agnosticism; which, unless stoical in its negative security, leads to an agonising longing for a word or a sign, for some indication of continued existence, some pledge that everything has not ceased, that love and memory still continue. This attitude, whatever view may be taken of religious observances and theological doctrines, is quite unnecessary in the light of scientific knowledge to-day. Doubtless it is a pardonable but it is an essentially feeble attitude. The strong position is to take sufficient pains to assure oneself, by critical examination of scientific evidence, what the facts really are; and then, when the crisis comes, to act upon that knowledge in full and assured conviction that all is well, and that wise and undemanding uncomplaining acquiescence has the power to make things still better.

The steadying, the strengthening, the almost exhilarating influence of this compact, in the present instance, was conspicuous. It broke the blow most effectively, it enabled the "gain of loss" to be realised to the full.

It was so, clearly, on this side; what of its effect on the other?

I say nothing about that at present, the time is not ripe; but those who know and are able to testify have on this subject no uncertain voice. Let that statement suffice for the present.

All that I permit myself to say further on what at present is considered to be the supernormal aspect of things, though it is really normal enough, is that it can all be understood as in simple harmony with orthodox teaching concerning "a cloud of witnesses" and the "communion of saints," and, further, that we in the body can be the source of an accession of strength to those in the Beyond; *Non sine nobis consummarentur.*

Whether supported on the wings of faith, or led along the more humdrum pathway of knowledge, most of us surely know that the departed are not wholly beyond our ken; and if so we should realise that those on the other side are grateful for our help. We may long for them to help us, but let us see to it that we help them. Be assured that they feel our attitude—love makes them sensitive; consciously or unconsciously we have an effect upon them—a strengthening or a debilitating effect; and amid the shock of surprise, the suddenness of untimely death, let us not fail them in all high endeavour to the utmost of our power.

In normal times the stress is far less severe. Old people pass away in the course of nature, prepared by experience and by feebleness of body for the transition. In such cases there need be no shock at all, but a peaceful reawakening with comparatively easy understanding of what has happened.

But amid the wholesale destruction caused by inhuman war, strong healthy vigorous lives are exploded into apparent nonentity; and unless they had some previous knowledge of what to expect, when they suddenly find themselves apart from their bodies and separated from their old surroundings, the experience may occasionally be an unnerving shock, an experience incredible and prostrating.

Hence the need for help—and many willing and active helpers on the other side undoubtedly there are. But it is open to us to help too. The future is indeed proverbially unknown to us, but insurance against its liabilities is possible; and so simple and easy an insurance against the shock of transition as the one here suggested, might be a widely prevalent precaution. All that is needed is a timely anticipation of what may happen, a compact between living friends as to their mutual attitude when to either the event occurs, and then a determination faithfully to execute each his part of the bargain.

The facts which establish persistence of existence or survival may not be generally known, but they lie open to investigation and are plain to those who seek. Some people seem to imagine, not only that there is no positive evidence, but that orthodox science has something definite to say *against* what is popularly called "immortality,"—as if there were some positive evidence against the possible survival of memory, character, and affection. There is nothing of the kind. There is no doubt plenty of evidence that the brain ceases to be available as an instrument, that the body as we know it returns to the earth whence it came. And the more this is emphasised in religious formularies, the better; for much semi-scientific prejudice against survival can probably trace its origin to the strange and repellent but venerable error that these material bodies are of permanent importance and will at some future time be resuscitated. Hence the phrase "resurrection of the body" often excites derision,—though it is known to be capable of interpretation in a serious and partially intelligible sense with a little ingenuity, as "resurrection body," σῶμα πνευματικόν, and in other similar ways familiar to theologians, but unfamiliar and alien to the biological and physical sciences.

It is manifest that many of these sciences are concerned specially with the physiological organism, its structure, function, specific energies, and nothing else; and to trouble specialists in those sciences with ideas about what happens after the death and destruction of this body is irrelevant and often irritating. Some of them, however, occasionally stray beyond the boundaries of their special field into the broader region of philosophy for a time, and there they are amenable to argument. But argument on broader lines is wasted on them while they remain purely physiological or biological workers in the narrow sense, while they are concerned only with the nature and properties of the material vehicle of life, and are not concerned with life itself.

A fact well known to philosophers is that even though, according to the views of leading physicists, the whole fabric of the material universe may gradually fall to destruction and return to cold or chaos, the immaterial entities of life and mind need share no such dissolution. But it is a fact that can never be verified in the dissecting room: its truth or otherwise must necessarily be established by psychological investigation. That biological science has, or ought to have, an open mind on subjects beyond its immediate and specialised ken can be illustrated from many distinguished writers, but I will content myself with appealing to a *clarum et venerabile nomen* and citing the cautious and tentative admission of Charles Darwin:—

"With respect to immortality, nothing shows me so clearly how strong and almost instinctive a belief it is as the consideration of the view now held by most physicists, namely, that the sun with all the planets will in time grow too cold for life, unless indeed some great body dashes into the sun, and thus gives it fresh life.

"Believing as I do that man in the distant future will be a far more perfect creature than he now is, it is an intolerable thought that he and all other sentient beings are doomed to complete annihilation after such long-continued slow progress. To those who fully admit the immortality of the human soul, the destruction of our world will not appear so dreadful."

There is a conservation of matter and of energy, there may be a conservation of life; or if not of life, of something which transcends life. I quote the assured utterance of a pioneer in psychic realms:

"No terrene Matter or Energy, but Love itself, is the imperishable of that higher world; so that earth's brief encounter with some spirit, quickly dear, may be the precursory omen of a far-off espousal, or the unconscious recognition of fond long-severed souls." [1]

And I solemnly believe that by our investigations into these at present dim regions we are preparing the way for apprehension of a truth which shall be universally recognised in the future.

"The humblest scouts who strive loyally to push forward the frontier of Science, even though Science at first disown them, are sure in time to hear her marching legions possess the unfrequented way."

[1] F. W. H. Myers, "Science and a Future Life."

SUPPLEMENT TO CHAPTER IV

In further illustration of the working of the scheme or compact now sufficiently explained, I am permitted to conclude this chapter by citing a few more private records, in order to show how the arrangement made a month or two before death was begun directly the event occurred, and how effectively and thoroughly it was executed.

The following brief private notes—some of them rough jottings on odd scraps of paper—were made from time to time by Christopher's Mother, mostly within a few days of the shock, the object being to record for her own use thoughts which came to her during "hours of insight," in the hope that they might aid in keeping her calm and steadfast, and concentrated in purpose, during any "hours of gloom" that might supervene.

By permission these private and personal notes are reproduced, solely in the hope that they may help others in like sorrow.

It was a very happy ending to the earthly part of a very happy life.

The impression I want to convey to him is this: that I know about his bodily death and the happy circumstances of it—that I accept this event as part of our mutual experience—that I share the whole in perfect companionship, ready and able to face and carry out my part of it, and knowing that for him it means *more* life and fuller.

He has won the Dark Tower, he has awakened from an ill dream and "across all this waste and desolate battlefield" he *has* attained to the haven where he would be.[1]

The one thing that could spoil it all for him is to see pain in my thoughts. He must see love and familiar greeting to his unchanged self, and nothing else: and his home must be full of happy thoughts about him.

"It is all right with me and all right with you; don't be troubled about me and I am *not* troubled about you—none of the conventional ideas about life and death meant anything to you and me, so we haven't got to get over anything; we can both of us know at once that we are each unchanged and as *close as ever*."

The fact that this experience deepens in me every conviction I ever had about life and death,—that my belief in "Love is all and Death is nought" absolutely stands the test of this shock and rending of my outer life,—is recognised by me.

Let me remember the words of . . . (a friend) written on the day her husband died: "Our long companionship here is broken and the deeper intimacy begun."

"In no strange land."

"God created man to be immortal and made him to be an image of *His own* eternity."

He had no fear of the act of death whatever—and not one shadow of doubt but that it was a physical event admitting his real self—unchanged—"just him"—into a more complete stage of life. He promised me not to think of me as over-come—but of me as that I should be knowing the main lines of his then situation, so that one factor of anxiety or worry should be entirely eliminated for him. We made sure that

[1] This refers to a passage in one of Christopher's last letters home, written before going into the Trenches (*see* page 255) :—

> "Well, the path lies before me. I feel like Childe Roland, and when I have won the Dark Tower—across all this waste and desolate battlefield—I shall return, please God, to 'the haven where I would be.' And I hope this time will soon come when we shall meet again and rejoice together."

whatever came we were already prepared for it, having mapped out what each was to do, and certain that each would proceed along the predetermined way.

I would not exchange the happiness of being his mother and having his companionship—the companionship of his dear mind—for anything this world has to offer. *What I have* is the thing to think of. "All that is at all, lasts ever."

A SONNET [1]

February 17th, 1918.

To all who wait, blindfolded by the flesh,
Upon the stammered promise that we give,
Tangling ourselves in the material mesh
A moment, while we tell you that we live,
Greeting, and reassurance; never doubt
That the slow tidings of our joyful state,
So hardly given, so haltingly made out,
Are but the creaking hinges of the gate. . . .
Beyond, the garden lies; and as we turn,
Wond'ring how much you hear, how much you guess,
Once more the roses of glad service burn
With hues of loving thought and thankfulness;
    Once more we move among them, strong and free,
    Marvelling yet in our felicity.

[1] This sonnet, obtained by "influenced" writing and attributed to the inspiration of F. W. H. M., is among certain material, not yet complete, which is coming through to the influenced writer and to others in the form of an account of the after-life. Assent has been given to the preliminary appearance of the sonnet in this place. It was not received by any relative of Christopher or Raymond, and has no specific connection with either.

PART II

MEMOIR
AUTOBIOGRAPHICAL FRAGMENT
AND
REPRESENTATIVE LETTERS

To that Immortal Company,
The Second Lieutenants aged 19
who fell in the Great War.
1914. . . .

―――――――

. . . Where our desires are and our hopes profound,
Felt as a well-spring that is hidden from sight,
To the innermost heart of their own land they are known
As the stars are known to the night;

As the stars that shall be bright when we are dust
Moving in marches upon the heavenly plain,
As the stars that are starry in the time of our darkness,
To the end, to the end, they remain.
                    LAURENCE BINYON, "For the Fallen."

CHAPTER V

By his Mother

"Sunshine was he
In the winter day;
And in the midsummer
Coolness and shade."
    From an Arab poem, quoted by Emerson
        in "Man the Reformer."

CHRISTOPHER TENNANT was born at Cadoxton Lodge in the Vale of Neath, on the 10th of October, 1897, the eldest child of his parents.

The story of his nineteen years of bodily life can be told in outline in a few words.

He went to a preparatory school (Mr. Helbert, West Downs, Winchester) in May, 1907, and remained there for four years. In 1911 he went on to Winchester (Kingsgate House, Mr. Beloe, and later Mr. Archibald Wilson), and was there until July, 1916, being then in Senior Division Sixth Book, and a School and House Prefect. He passed into Sandhurst as a Prize Cadet, and passing out in April, 1917, was gazetted to the Welsh Guards. He joined his Regiment early in May, and crossed to France with a draft on August 9th. At dawn on the morning of September 3rd he fell in action in the trenches near Langemarck, at the age of 19 years and 10 months.

His childhood was chiefly spent in the old Welsh home to which he was so passionately devoted. Cadoxton Lodge is an ancient rambling white-washed manor-house lying near the mouth of the Vale of Neath, a valley famous for its beauty, its woods, its waterfalls, its guardian ranges of hills. The house itself is surrounded by one of those old-world gardens where old-fashioned flowers lift year by year familiar faces in the same spot. The large walled kitchen garden is not so much an adjunct to as an integral part of the flower garden, from the fact that a terrace walk some two hundred yards long stretches past the house and on through the kitchen garden to a bright patch of flowers and an ivy-canopied seat. The house faces south, wreathed in vine and climbing rose. On this front grows what is said to be the largest magnolia tree in Wales, the girth of the bole being over 55 inches. From August onwards it bears a wealth of large white blossoms, flowers whose heavy scent pervades both house and garden. The ancient lead waterpipes and cisterns date probably from the seventeenth century. The cisterns are decorated with the figure of Time holding a scythe, and the pipes with floral designs intermingled with leopards' heads and the face of a man blowing a drapery from his half-open mouth.

Beyond the garden and meadow the Vale spreads out across to the beautiful rounded hills which close it in

freer than that of sense. Her influence spurred him to live at his best, to be in the root of him honest and true and good. The sense of her unseen presence gilded the grey hours of loneliness which school life was soon to bring, and forged an ever closer link between Mother and Son.

The writer does not think that after the first shock this experience saddened his life, but it certainly enriched it, and gave him an outlook on life and death which the first touch of early manhood found unshaken and powerful to guide and to control.

The happiness of those nursery days returned to him in a great measure through the birth of two small brothers, Alexander, born 1909, and Henry, known to his intimates as "The Wise One," born 1913. The difference in age between him and these two small folk made his relationship to them almost a fatherly one. What he meant to them and what they meant to him is not dwelt on here.

Another influence—not indeed separate from that of the little sister's, rather springing from and bound up with the thought of her—came to him about this time.

Frederic Myers, the poet and psychologist, whose name is for ever identified with Psychical Research, was his uncle by marriage. He died when Christopher was 3½ years old, and it is certain that the child had no recollection of him. But he became a living reality in the boy's life. To hear him speak of "Fred" was to realise at once that a kinship of spirit, some inexplicable affinity of soul, existed between them. Their tastes were not dissimilar. Frederic Myers' love of the Classics found a reflection, as time passed, in Christopher's mind. Both shared to the full the love of Nature in its wilder aspects, and of poetry; both were haunted by visions of

> "Something far more deeply interfused,
> Whose dwelling is the light of setting suns,
> And the round ocean and the living air,
> And the blue sky, and in the mind of man:
> A motion and a spirit, that impels
> All thinking things, all objects of all thought,
> And rolls through all things . . ."

both had a vivid interest in the question of what death means to human personality.

As Christopher grew up he became well read in Frederic Myers' works, both prose and poetry. From the age of 15 onwards he bought and studied many books on telepathy, clairvoyance, and dreams. It was perhaps because he himself was such an absolutely healthy-minded, cheerful, efficient creature that he could do this without anyone thinking it strange. The publications of the Society for Psychical Research (of which he was never a member) were eagerly devoured when they came his way. From 1912 onwards his close friendship with the family of Mr. Gerald Balfour (President of the S. P. R. 1906-1907) brought him into contact with men and women who had made a study of that branch of science with which the Society concerns itself. He became a diligent reader of Sir Oliver Lodge's books. He discussed with his Mother, sometimes far into the night, the problems raised by these matters and their bearing on life in general; but it was always the thought of the little sister that lay at the back of his mind. Before his death he had attained a complete conviction that life and love and memory survive the grave, and before he sailed for France he spoke of the possibility of his falling in battle, and arranged with his Mother exactly what her actions, and his, would be after his death, if this occurred.

Christopher was always a great reader. From the time he was ten years old onwards he read omnivorously. Reading aloud was a part of the daily round of the life of his family, and by this means he laid hold of a large portion of that great inheritance of English Literature which our children may possess for the asking. Even in those early days Blake, Tennyson, Browning, Wordsworth were becoming old friends, and from the age of fifteen onwards he read much poetry under whatever circumstances he found himself.

His love of music was also marked. He never missed the chance of hearing classical music, and would often quote the saying, "He who has heard the Fifth Symphony has known the mind of Beethoven." London, and to some extent Winchester, afforded him the opportunities he prized, but it was a humble instrument —no more than a pianola—that gave him the larger part of his first-hand knowledge of the works of his two special divinities, Beethoven and Wagner. The long sunlit summer afternoons and the long winter evenings which he spent at the pianola in the Music

Room at Cadoxton—a large white-walled room with high vaulted roof, perfect for sound—were among the happiest of his life. He played the pianola with great skill, and got an immense amount out of this Cinderella of musical instruments. To hear it played by another was to realise this at once.

No picture of the boy would be complete which omitted to mention his invincible gaiety of spirits, his keen sense of fun (degenerating in earlier days into a habit of practical joking, which was sternly repressed by outraged "grown-ups"), his love of amusement and good company, his powers of mimicry (the latter much appreciated by the annual "private theatricals" party, in which he always took a leading rôle, usually dying with shocking realism under the blow of a home-made cardboard dagger), his love of the theatre, his delight in impromptu entertainments, and his affection for the ices of Gunter, the consuming of which in the Berkeley Square rooms took on by degrees an almost ritual significance for him and his mother. Up to the last Christmas the fiction of the visit of Father Christmas to fill expectant stockings was maintained between them. The small socks gave place to hand-knit stockings, and these again to capacious shooting stockings, the filling of which in the dead of night became an increasingly difficult problem.

At the age of 9 a great upheaval came into the boy's life. The inexorable law of custom as it exists in his caste drew him from the sunny valley of home up into the bleak pass of school life. It was inevitable that he should feel the change acutely, and equally inevitable that, given his temperament and tastes, school life should have remained to him throughout as something alien to his spirit.

The fragment of autobiography which he has left gives something of this sense of a being "moving about in worlds not realised." The sense of the irksomeness of many of the features of school life gave place, to some extent, to one of real enjoyment when at Winchester he reached a place in the school which brought him into close relation with such men as Mr. Frank Carter and the Head Master, Mr. Montague Rendall. To say that he delighted in them would be no exaggeration. He loved, too, the beauty of the old buildings, of the great Cathedral—which by some strange freak of the Powers that Be was "out of bounds" when he first entered the school—of the views from Hills [1]; and he became linked in ties of close friendship with some of the men in his house, more especially after he had become a prefect.

But it is true to say that having "gone through the mill" himself, he maintained a critical attitude towards the Public School system as he had known it. Those who wish to follow this point further are advised to read that powerful novel written by a schoolboy, "The Loom of Youth," by Alec Waugh. The writer received a few painful letters dealing with this side of school

[1] St. Catherine's Hill, about three-quarters of a mile from the College, a place associated with ancient school customs, of which names-calling twice a year still survives.

life, written from 1913 onwards, but looking back she cannot regret that her son was a rebel (not for nothing was he ninth in direct' descent from Oliver Cromwell) against the established order of things as it exists in Public Schools. It gave him a sturdiness of character and an independence of outlook which prevented him from drifting, and the experience was no doubt wholesome.

"... welcome each rebuff
That turns Earth's smoothness rough,
Each sting that bids nor sit nor stand but go!"

His visions of a life at Trinity College, Cambridge, of which he became a member, but which he never actually entered, melted away before the actualities of the Great War. Having realised that he had "got to be a soldier," as he expressed it, it was characteristic of him that he should wish to learn his job thoroughly. Military life seemed to offer him nothing congenial; he certainly was not inspired by any hatred of the German people, and the whole business of war appeared to him to be as wearisome as it was horrible. But the call, once given, was nobly responded to. His classical work was set aside without a murmur, "working for marks" —a form of occupation he always despised—was carried on up to the eve of the Sandhurst entrance examination, and once he entered the R.M.C. he laid his uphill shoulder to the wheel and put his whole energy into the round of work there, remote as it was from all that had hitherto occupied his mind.

Much in the atmosphere of Sandhurst was uncongenial. The vast number of youths of different education and different traditions gathered together there meant inevitable friction. The lack of any human relation between the officials and the individual cadets, the monotony of the life, the strenuous physical exertion, often beyond what is wise for boys of 18, the occasional outbursts of rowdiness—all these things were displeasing. But there was gold amid the grey. He thoroughly enjoyed the society of some kindred spirits in his Company (K Company, stationed in the Old Buildings), and in particular he rejoiced in the friendship of Peter Harris [1], whom he had known in early childhood.

In April, 1917, Christopher passed out of Sandhurst, twelfth on the list, and on April 30th he was gazetted to the Welsh Guards.

To understand what this meant to him it is necessary to say a few words about his passionate pride in the land of his birth and in the Welsh people. Though sprung from a stock predominantly English, he had a strain of pure Welsh blood in him on his mother's side. He counted himself wholly a Welshman, and nationality for him meant Welsh nationality. He loved the Welsh people with an understanding love which is denied to the Saxon. He understood their faults, he perceived their spiritual and intellectual qualities, he responded to their quick-hearted likes and dislikes. His relations with the dwellers on the property of his fam-

[1] 2nd-Lieut. P. E. C. Harris, 3rd Battalion, Coldstream Guards.

ily were particularly happy. A strong democrat, he never posed as "the young squire"—indeed, one of the characteristics which won for him so wide a circle of friends in such different walks of life was his habit of utterly ignoring barriers of class, education, and even of sex, and of valuing individuals for what they were in themselves as human beings. In his dealing with others—even casual acquaintances, old people, humble folk, children, servants—the human note was always struck. Each was made to feel that he or she counted for him as an end in himself or herself, and not as a means to any other end. The fact that his mother was engaged in public work of various kinds, work in which he always helped when at home, brought a great variety of people into his home. He was thrown into contact with many men whom he might otherwise have missed, Labour men, Welsh-speaking Free Churchmen, Trades Unionists, politicians of all the three great parties in the State. This contact enlarged his sympathies and provided him with a training that would have been of value to his country—that great South Wales coalfield which is the cock-pit of democracy—had he been spared to devote himself to a life spent in her service.

In politics he was keenly interested, and political discussions were part of the atmosphere in which he was reared, partly due to the fact that while his Father leaned towards a Toryism of the old school, his Mother was what a friend described, more in sorrow than in wrath, as "a fanatical Liberal."

Thus it was that his joining the Welsh Guards filled him with profound satisfaction. Here were his own people, and he felt that he belonged to them, that their God was his God also. The sound of the first bars of their National Air, "Hen Wlad fy Nhadau" ("Dear Land of my Fathers"), always brought him leaping to his feet, the sight of the Red Dragon on the Welsh Flag meant more to him than all the Union Jacks that were ever woven, the National Eisteddfod stood to him as a great religious Festival. Of all the sons of Wales who have laid their gift upon the altar, none has loved her more deeply and more passionately than he.

He joined the Welsh Guards in May. The regiment was then stationed at Tadworth, and from the first day down to the very last his life with his regiment was one of unmixed happiness.

The writer is not sufficiently familiar with the atmosphere of military life to know whether all the friendliness, good-comradeship, and affection which was showered upon her son was such as falls to the lot of every subaltern. She only knows that his delight in his brother officers, his pride in his men, his satisfaction in finding that he "knew his job," his sense of having come into a united family who loved him and whom he loved —all this made those last months of his bodily life a time of complete happiness. It was enough to look at him to know that this was so.

He had inherited the brown hair and the large gentle brown eyes of his Welsh great-grandmother; his six-feet-three-inches of straight young manhood seemed to radiate joy. He was very good to look upon in his various uniforms, and this too pleased him, as a new toy may please a merry child.

And it was not only life at Tadworth that he found sweet. London was easy of access, and London, when one is young, heart-whole, and well provided with funds, is a place of great possibilities. Dinner parties at the Berkeley followed by a play, and sometimes, regardless of food economy, by supper at the Savoy or the Carlton, were of frequent occurrence. The Guards' Club gave him the rendezvous he needed, and his grandmother's house [1] under the shadow of the Houses

---

[1] His grandmother, Gertrude Barbara Rich Tennant, only survived him by a few months, dying in April, 1918, in the ninety-ninth year of her age. She was the eldest daughter of Vice-Admiral Henry T. B. Collier, and through her mother, Harriet Nicholas of Aston Keynes, traced her descent direct from Oliver Cromwell. Born in 1819, the first twenty-four years of her life were spent almost entirely in France, where as a girl she became intimately acquainted with all that was distinguished in the literary, artistic and social world of Paris. Gustave Flaubert, Alphonse Daudet, Gambetta, Renan, and many others of note were numbered among her friends, and to the last she retained a warm admiration for French ways of life and thought, the experiences of her early days having, indeed, stamped her whole personality with something of the charm and distinction of the great ladies of the *ancien régime.* Her remarkable beauty and quick intelligence won for her a ready welcome in London when at the age of 24 she returned to England. Not long afterwards she married Charles Tennant, of Cadoxton Lodge, for many years Member for St. Albans, a man of outstanding ability and strength of character, with strong democratic sympathies and a forward-looking mind. Of the children of this marriage, Dorothy married H. M. Stanley, the explorer, Eveleen became the wife of Frederic Myers the poet and psychologist, and the only son, Charles Coombe Tennant, is the father of the subject of this Memoir by his marriage with Winifred, daughter of Lieut. George Pearce-Serocold, R.N. (*See* p. 137.)

Mrs. Tennant's *salon* at her house in Whitehall was for long the meeting place of a wide circle of interesting people, including

of Parliament was always open to him. Certain of the special courses of instruction which he went through necessitated residence in London, and then his Father or his Mother usually joined him, and all the amusements became doubly delightful.

In July his only London dance, one given by a brother officer to whom he was especially attached, caught him just before he was sent abroad. There he danced most of the evening with a lovely and unknown damsel to whom he had never been introduced, and whose name he never discovered. His attitude towards women was always perfect—perhaps the result of his having been reared in a home where belief in the equality of the sexes, and the equality of opportunity which forms its natural corollary, had always been an article of faith.

The letters written during the brief time he was on

such great Victorians as John Bright, Gladstone, Ruskin, Tennyson, Huxley, Herbert Spencer, George Eliot, Watts, Burne-Jones, and many others. Though already 78 years of age at the time of Christopher's birth, the relation between them was not so much one of youth and age as of mutual affection and admiration. She was essentially one of those people who do not date. Up to the time of his death she retained her memory and all her faculties unimpaired, and took a keen interest in the doings of the world at large. Age had done little to rob her of the beauty of feature and colouring for which she had been famous; she seemed gifted with perennial youth. She remained a vivid and arresting human being, full of individual traits, and joining, as it were, in her own person two different epochs of European history—for she had danced as a child in Paris at the Court of Charles X. (1824-1830), and she lived to see the three great battles of Ypres in the present war (1914-1917). Pre-eminently gifted by nature herself, she was quick to recognise and appreciate ability in others, and her interest and pride in Christopher, to whom she looked to carry on a high tradition of family history, was a marked feature of her later years.

active service in France and Flanders which are included in the present volume, speak for themselves. He
enjoyed "the great adventure," and before he had seen
anything of the darker side of war he was lifted as by
an invisible hand into that world which held for him
the welcoming eyes of his sister, the little sister beneath whose name in his locked MS. book he had
written:

"Experta vitæ consitum spinis iter,
Clausit tenellum lumen, et vidit Deum." [1]

It was but a little way and into a familiar country
that he passed.

[Here ends his mother's Memoir.]

[1] Mr. Ernest Myers kindly supplies the following translation:

"Life's thorny way she for a moment trod,
Closed her sweet infant eyes, and looked on God."

"*Tenellum*," he adds, "is a diminutive of *tenerum* (tender), and
perhaps needs the two words I have used to express it. I never saw
these touching lines before and would much like to know where they
are to be found. Probably they are a Christian epitaph."

SUPPLEMENT TO CHAPTER V

American readers may be interested to know that the subject of this book had a strain of American blood in him and was descended from a lady who held a prominent place in the social life of South Carolina in the early part of the XVIII Century. His Great-great-great Grandmother was Miss Sarah Rhett of Charleston, South Carolina (born 1725; died 1808), who, in 1743, at the age of eighteen, married Admiral Sir Thomas Frankland, 5th Bart., of Thirkleby, Yorkshire, at Charleston. She was the daughter of John Rhett (son of Col. William Rhett, Lt. Governor of South Carolina and Vice Admiral of the Navy) by Mary Trott his wife. Both her parents dying in 1728, within a few days of each other, of fever, when Sarah was but three years old, she was brought up by her Maternal Grandfather, Chief Justice Nicholas Trott, at his home The Point, near Charleston. Nicholas Trott had settled in that town in 1690, and he exercised a dominating influence in the Colony. As judge, it fell to his lot to try the notorious Captain Kidd and his associates, who were arrested in Boston, Mass., in July, 1699. Kidd had been sent out as a Privateer in 1690, but was eventually arrested as a pirate, by Col. William Rhett, and sent to England, where he was hanged in 1704. Sarah Rhett's paternal Grandfather, Col. William Rhett (born 1666, died 1722), also occupied an important position in South Carolina. He was a Lieut.-General of Militia, Commissioner of Customs for Carolina, and Surveyor General. He was also Vice-Admiral of the Navy, and distinguished himself in various Naval engagements against the Spanish and French. The Rhett family Vault is in St. Philip's Churchyard, Charleston, South Carolina, and is embellished with the Rhett coat of arms "Or, a cross engrailed, sable."

Sarah Rhett left America in 1744, after her marriage, and resided in England until her death in 1808, at the age of eighty-two. A portrait of this lady, painted when she was about twenty-three years of age, is now in the possession of the Tennant family, whose descent from her is shown in the accompanying table.

Admiral Sir Thomas Frank-=Sarah Rhett of Charleston, land, 5th Bart. M.P., b. South Carolina, b. 1725; d. 1718; m. 1743; d. 1784. 1808. Her great-grand-He descended from Frances, father, Sir Walter Rhett, is 4th daughter of Oliver said to have accompanied Cromwell. Charles II from the Hague to England (1660).

Charlotte, 7th daughter, b.=Robert Nicholas, of Ashton 1760; m. 1778; d. 1800. Keynes, Wilts; M.P., F.S. A.; Chairman of the Board of Excise for upwards of 32 years; b. 1758; d. 1826.

Harriet, 4th daughter, b.=Vice-Admiral Henry T. B. 1793; m. 1816; d. 1850. Collier, 4th son of Admiral Sir George Collier, M.P., and younger brother of Ad-miral Sir Francis Collier; C.B., K.L.S., K.C.H., b. 1791; d. 1872.

Gertrude Barbara Rich, eld-=Charles Tennant, M.P., D.L., est daughter, b. 1819; m. co: Glam., of Cadoxton 1847; d. 1918. She was Lodge, Neath, South 7th in direct descent from Wales, b. 1796; d. 1873. Oliver Cromwell.

Charles Coombe Tennant, =Winifred, daughter of Lieut. J.P. of Cadoxton Lodge, George Pearce-Serocold, only son; m. 1895. R.N.

George Christopher Serocold Tennant, eldest son, Second Lieutenant 1st Battalion Welsh Guards, b. 1897. Killed in action in Flanders 1917.

CHAPTER VI

". . . Even then I felt
Gleams like the flashing of a shield:—the Earth
And common face of Nature spake to me
Rememberable things."

WORDSWORTH, Prelude, II.

IN October 1911, on Christopher's fourteenth birthday, his mother gave him a book for manuscript, bound in red leather and fitted with a lock and key. The contents of this book remained unknown to her until she read them in September, 1917, after her son's death. Here follow some extracts:—

Tadworth Camp, July, 1917.

This is not an attempt at autobiography—it is merely an attempt to set down a few incidents of my past life, an attempt which, writing as I do at the age of 19 years 9 months, must necessarily be incomplete and lacking in detail. But whether I survive this war or not it may be of interest both for myself and for those dear to me to have some record of things which may not linger in my memory. I shall write from time to time as the spirit moves me, not striving for flow of expression, but setting down simply what comes into my mind—here as I sit at Tadworth Camp in my tent, with the sun streaming in upon me and the voices of my fellow officers sounding in the distance.

Like the lives of most other men, mine falls into periods: Before school—Private school—Public school —Sandhurst—the Army. I was born at Cadoxton on October 10th, 1897. My childhood was, I think, on the whole very happy, chiefly because of the love that has existed between my parents (harsh word!) and myself—yes, ever since I can remember. I know now that I was born into the world almost inanimate— and that the doctor restored life by judicious flapping with wet towels. My earliest recollection is of watching a snow storm at the age of about 4, standing on a chair in my nursery at Cadoxton with old Nurse beside me. Then, as I got a little older, my Father and Mother went off to Algiers, and old Nurse wrote daily that "Master Christopher eats well, sleeps well, and takes his food"!

Cadoxton was a house full of mystery to me, and though never afraid I was visited on two occasions by strange fancies—so vividly did they impress themselves on my mind that they remain clear till this day. The psychology of them must be interesting. The first happened when I was about 5 years old—the second a few days afterwards. I was lying in my bed in my nursery, and old Nurse was sitting in a chair by the fire. There was also a lamp in the room. I had only just been put in bed when I had the feeling of being watched, and looking towards the door I was under the impression that it opened and shut noiselessly. (The sequence of this is interesting.) Then I seemed to distinguish above the screen in the corner, a screen which partially surrounded the door but did not totally conceal the top of it from my bed—above the screen, I say, appeared a forehead and eyes—the top part of a face, in fact. The face was black, and two black eyes watched me. My instinct was to duck under the clothes, but with immense effort and prompted by curiosity I resisted the instinct. The next thing I saw was a long black neck shooting out over the top of the screen, with a black shapeless face at the end of it. Then I did duck under the clothes. This by itself might have been a bad dream, or a trick of the shadows, but the curious thing is that a few days—or it may have been weeks—afterwards the following occurred. It was the afternoon, between lunch and tea, and I was sitting on the ground with old Nurse sewing beside me. She had given me a large box of old Christmas cards to play with, and I had arranged them, standing them up, all over the nursery floor—no one could have walked from the door to the window without upsetting some of them. Suddenly, without any warning, I saw coming from the door a figure, clothed in black close-fitting draperies, with the same black face I had seen before, though the hands were whiter. The figure came towards me with a trotting gait, walked *through* all the Christmas cards without upsetting any, till it reached the window; then it turned and trotted back, disappearing as it got towards the door. The door never opened, and old Nurse seemed, as far as I can remember, to notice nothing unusual. My feelings were entirely those of interest and curiosity at being thus able to identify this visitant with the one of a former occasion—and prove to myself that it had been

CHRISTOPHER WITH HIS DOG BOXER.
OCTOBER, 1900. AGED 3 YEARS.

no dream. I felt not a shadow of fear, but somehow I have never spoken of these things.

So much for my early recollections of Cadoxton, where I used to spend six months of the year. The other six were spent in London at 5, Sloane Court, in Lower Sloane Street. I can remember very early days there—I can still conjure up the peculiar smell of the cupboards—those white cupboards in the nursery, the Red Room where Deedooge [1] used to read to me, Mother's room with Japanese prints, and the dining-room from which I watched the naturalist's shop below, and the sentry in his red coat and bearskin outside Chelsea Barracks. These things seem very far away, as in a dream. One morning—I was very young—my Mother called me to her room, and said, "Carry this thought in your mind to-day—'God is love.' " I have always remembered that.

Many incidents I have forgotten. Innumerable governesses I remember as concrete things, but the general impression of my first years in London left me with memories of sunlit days in the Chelsea Gardens, and a sweet glamour of childhood associated with the scent of white hawthorn and the songs of thrushes in the trees.

It is strange, what I have called the glamour of childhood—those gardens that seemed to me full of a celestial brightness—the essential happiness and joy of my life. Delicious shady nooks were there which seemed like a paradise to me, full of the sound of cooing doves and the smell of spring, delicious scents

[1] A name given by Christopher as a small child to his Father, which became a permanent addition to the family vocabulary.

floating from the flower gardens, the whole world trans-figured with celestial light. I feel intensely that that which Wordsworth sets down in his "Ode on the Intimations of Immortality" has been my actual experience. I knew those clouds of glory in my childhood, I felt them fading with boyhood, and now I feel those fancies "pass away and fade into the light of common day." Yet there are certain things which bring them back to me, and recall that glamour and splendour of the past—sunset, and the song of birds, and Thompson's "Ode to the Setting Sun"—such things bring back to me what now seems "desolate sweetness far and far away." How my childhood invested these places with a divine glory, and how small and sordid they now seem, returning after an interval of some years! Strange indeed!

London, too, impressed me. How vast, how full of people it seemed! I remember so well going to bed by candlelight, and waking in the morning with the light streaming through the windows. I remember the curious effect on the ceiling of cabs and lighted vehicles passing at night, arms of light shooting across the ceiling from the top of the window and travelling slowly across it. I remember parties, too,—with Peter [1] and others—and I remember my Mother, a vision of beauty in her low dress, with pearl necklaces and diamond tiara—and my Father, who used to give me a lighted candle to blow out, to comfort me, and used to sit beside my bed when I could not go to sleep. Vaguely, too, comes back the memory of measles, and

[1] Peter Harris, afterwards at Sandhurst with him, and now a Second-Lieutenant in the Coldstream Guards.

of how ill I was, and how I could hardly walk when I first got up afterwards.

Then came our expedition to France. How I loved France—the Riviera, with its blue sky, and beds of violets, and mimosa trees! We travelled right through to Marseilles, and I slept in the train and woke up at Lyons. We went to Hyères. There was a lovely garden there, belonging to the Abbé, full of flowers and bees.

INTERPOLATION

[Christopher's acquaintance with this garden and with the Abbé Marquand—who became so good a friend to him—occurred in the following way.

Stevenson's "Child's Garden of Verse" had been a familiar companion from very early days, and his usual desire to know something of the people who had written the things he cared for led his Mother to read the Life of R. L. S. and the two volumes of his Letters edited by Sidney Colvin.

When the family party reached Hyères their first thought was of the villa in which R. L. S. had lived from the spring of 1883 for the greater part of sixteen months. The "Child's Garden of Verse," "The Silverado Squatters," and "Black Arrow" belong to this period. Writing in October, 1883, R. L. S. describes his house thus:—"My address is still the same, and I live in a most sweet corner of the universe; sea and fine hills before me, and a rich variegated plain; at my back a craggy hill, loaded with vast feudal ruins. I am very quiet; a person passing by my door half startles me; but I enjoy the most aromatic airs, and at night the most wonderful view into a moonlit garden. By day this garden fades into nothing, overpowered by its surroundings and the luminous distance; but at night, and when the moon is out, that garden, the arbour, the flight of stairs that mount the artificial hillock, the plumed blue gum-trees that hang trembling, become the very skirts of Paradise. Angels I know frequent it; and it thrills all night with the flutes of silence."

It was in this same garden that the problem of the disposal of an army of snails collected by R. L. S. arose: "Our lovely garden is a prey to snails; I have gathered about a bushel, which, not having the heart to slay, I steal forth withal and deposit near my neighbour's garden wall. As a case of casuistry, this presents many points of interest. I loathe the snails, but from loathing to actual butchery, trucidation of multitudes, there is a step that I hesitate to take. What then to do with them? My neighbour's vineyard, pardy! It is a rich villa pleasure garden, of course; if it were a peasant's patch the snails I suppose would have to perish."

This story always amused Christopher, and to enter and explore this garden was one of the fixed determinations of his days at Hyères. His Mother thought it wise to go and spy out the land alone as a preliminary step. The following is taken from a contemporary note made by her at Hyères in March 1905:—

"It was not without emotion that I first beheld the little house. Set back behind a wooden paling, the white-washed chalet with its overhanging eaves lay like a white bird against the background of verdure. On the ground were three long French windows opening on to a little tile-paved path from whence on either side a flight of steps led up into the garden. Above, the wooden balcony ran round three sides of the house, the windows of the upper floor opening out upon it. The whole impression was one of a harmony of white and brown; white walls making a setting for the note of brown in the carved woodwork of balcony, eave, and window frame.

"At the back rose the garden, bright with flowering shrubs; and far above, the half-ruined tower of the old château kept watch like a forgotten sentinel.

"Not without some misgiving I crossed the road and pulled the bell that hung just outside the *grille*. The sound of footsteps came from the garden path, and in another moment I found myself face to face with the occupant of *La Solitude*.[1]

"I do not know exactly whom I had expected to find living in Stevenson's house, but it was certainly not the priest who, in cassock and biretta, now opened the door and let me in. He was a man verging on middle age, dark, of medium height,

---

[1] The name of the villa.

with intelligent and kindly eyes that reassured me at once. He led me through an open window on the ground floor into a tiny study, set me at my ease in a few moments, and was soon asking a hundred eager questions about Stevenson, of whom he had heard as 'ce grand écrivain étranger qui habitait ici autrefois.' My interview with M. l'Abbé was a most happy one. It seemed strange to be speaking of R. L. S. in what had probably been his own writing-room. I tried to give some incomplete picture of the compelling charm of his character, of his joyous blitheness of spirit, persisting even in the darkest days, of his intuitive sympathy with all forms of life, and of the deep and abiding effect he has had upon many who never knew him.

"Then M. l'Abbé rose and led me from room to room. The real entrance is from the back of the chalet and leads directly on to the upper story, from whence a miniature staircase descends to the ground floor. On the latter are two sitting-rooms, very diminutive and very cheerful, the kitchen and pantry. Above are four bedrooms opening on to the balcony. Everywhere I saw evidence of the most refined and cultivated taste; a note of ordered simplicity prevailed; the walls were coloured in delicate neutral shades, and formed an admirable background for some fine pieces of ancient walnut furniture and old oil paintings in heavily carved frames. The little dwelling was very flower-like, very reposeful—full of sweetness and light. We passed out into the garden and along the winding paths edged with narcissus, violets, and roses, with aloes and fresias: flowers everywhere, such as one only sees in a garden where none are ever picked and each plant may bear its full load of blossom undisturbed. Everywhere, too, birds, as in the days more than twenty years ago when R. L. S. wrote of the 'fair wood music in this solitude of ours.' In one corner stood a gnarled old olive tree half buried in falling honeysuckle; the terrace that runs along the garden's upmost slope is bordered by fine aloes; and a mimosa in full bloom—a veritable firework of falling gold—brought a vivid note of colour into the scene.

"A flight of stone steps leads up to what was once a studio, now transformed into an oratory in which M. l'Abbé daily celebrates Mass. The dim light and perfect ·silence of the little chapel had something of mystery and peace as I passed into it from the bird-haunted sun-bathed garden. Above the altar rose a figure of the Saviour, around it great bowls of mimosa were grouped, filling the air with a subtle perfume; on either side stood a smaller statue, to the right the Virgin Mother, to the left Joseph with his carpenter's tools. The consecration of many prayers brooded like a benediction above the spot. . . . This was the beginning of a close friendship between us, for nothing could have exceeded the exquisite hospitality of the Abbé to me, a stranger not only in race but also in creed. It was the story of Crocket and the Bishop of El Seo over again, told with such subtle charm in 'A Wayfarer in Spain.' I later knew that my Abbé of *La Solitude* belonged also to that never very numerous company of human souls that stand outside and above every accident of race and creed and century; that link us with the great *Illuminati* of the past, and renew, in hearts grown weary with the complexity of life, the glow of faith in Man's destiny."

Thus it came about that Christopher was made free of the lovely garden of his dreams during several happy weeks. A letter on page 289 shows how close the link between the boy and his French friend remained.]

Autobiographical Fragment Resumed.

Then came The Darling. I will not speak much of her. She was a very living person to me, and I still feel her a living influence in my life. God bless her. Some day we shall meet and look into each other's eyes, for the love between us is great. I remember her so well. She was so beautiful and so unique, and meant so much to me.

In 1907 I went to West Downs, a preparatory school near Winchester. I was very unhappy and very homesick at first, but it all helped me to gain that *savoir faire* that enables one to get on with men. That is the most that can be said of it. At first I was entirely out of my element. The boys just above me bullied me and the others of my lot. I found my feet as I got on, and liked the place eventually. It was a clean school, though full of intrigues and petty spite, as schools are. The masters were very nice men; Helbert was a good teacher, and made the school run well, and made his boys as happy as they might be under such circumstances.

Personally I have always been a lover of freedom, and have resented the control of *all* my actions by vengeful deities. That control is necessary, I know, but it can be done with wise love, and it can be done in a spirit of smug prudery; and it is very often done in the latter. Perhaps I misjudged authority and thought harshly of it in those days, but moments of freedom and leisure made up to a large extent for the constant supervision. There is a certain kind of old-maidishness which makes my blood boil, and I have always thought it latent in most schoolmasters. However, I am now inclined to think they are more like ordinary people, and assume a rôle which they imagine to be suitable for dealing with the young.

I thought West Downs at first what I should call "hard," perhaps owing to the absence of carpets and other amenities of civilised life. The place was bare, the people's minds were bare. I noted at the time, without being able to express it, a certain mental inelasticity and absence of imagination in the people there. I was intensely romantic by nature then, and found no corresponding chord in my superiors. They were nice, but unsympathetic.

Apart from this criticism, I had a pleasant time the last few years at West Downs—at least, I sometimes feel that it was rather a grey stretch of vague indefiniteness, with pleasant moments and incidents dotted here and there. But I do not think one minds so much at the time, as on looking back at it afterwards.

[*Here the fragment of autobiography breaks off.*]

The locked MS. book (called by Christopher his Red Book) also contains a small number of other entries, made on different dates prior to that of the above Autobiographical Fragment. Of these the following only are quoted as showing their general character:—

"Dearly beloved and longed for, my joy and crown, so stand fast in the Lord, my dearly beloved." [1]

TABLET IN KESWICK CHURCH. [2]

In Memory of Frederic William Henry Myers.
Eldest son of the Rev. Frederic Myers.
Born at Keswick February 8th, 1843.
Departed this life at Rome, January, 1901.

"He asked life of Thee, and Thou gavest him a long life, even for ever and ever."

May 1st, 1916.

"To God again the enfranchised soul must tend,
He is her home; her Author is her End.
Hers is no death; when earthly eyes grow dim
Starlike she soars, and Godlike melts in Him." [3]

F. W. H. M.

---

[1] From Philippians iv. 1. These words are on a brass tablet placed below a Della Robbia bas-relief in the church of St. Cattwg, Cadoxton-juxta-Neath, in memory of his sister.

[2] Visited by Christopher in September, 1912.

[3] A translation of Georgics iv., 223, by Frederic Myers. See the Essay on Virgil, "Classical Essays," p. 174.

Οὔ μ' ἔτι, παρθενικαὶ μελιγάρυες ἱμερόφωνοι,
γυῖα φέρην δύναται. βάλε δὴ βάλε κηρύλος εἴην,
ὅστ' ἐπὶ κύματος ἄνθος ἀμ' ἀλκυόνεσσι ποτῆται
νηδεὲς ἦτορ ἔχων, ἀλιπόρφυρος εἴαρος ὄρνις.[1]

[1] "No longer, sweetly murmuring loving-voiced maidens, my limbs can support me. Would, ah! would that I were a Kingfisher who along the flower of the wave flits with the halcyons, his heart at ease, the sea-blue bird of Spring."

ALCMAN.

CHAPTER VII

WEST DOWNS

"Thus encircled by the mystery of Existence; under the deep heavenly Firmament; waited on by the four golden Seasons, with their vicissitudes of contribution . . . did the Child sit and learn. . . .

"Nevertheless I were but a vain dreamer to say that even then my felicity was perfect. I had, once for all, come down from Heaven into the Earth. Among the rainbow colours that glowed on my horizon, lay even in childhood a dark ring of Care, as yet no thicker than a thread, and often quite overshone. . . . It was the ring of Necessity whereby we are all begirt; happy he for whom a kind heavenly Sun brightens it into a ring of Duty, and plays round it with beautiful prismatic diffractions; yet ever, as basis and bourne of our whole being, it is there."   CARLYLE, "Sartor Resartus."

In May, 1907, Christopher's school life began. He went in that month to West Downs (Mr. Helbert), a preparatory school, which lies high above the ancient city of Winchester and looks out over a wide stretch of rolling country. Here he was to remain for the next four years. At the time there were between fifty and sixty boys in the school. I am indebted to his Parents for these and all other details.

West Downs, May, 1907.
My dear Mum,—I drink tea for tea and tea for breakfast! It is difficult to get time to write to you,

because there is such a lot of changing for cricket, and
then I *have* to go out, and lessons, etc.

The Matron puts my bath ready. There are many
boys younger than me here. I like my Pater[1] very
well. My Pater just arrived when I did, so he does
not know much himself. We go to chapel every morning and evening. . . . The lark woke me up this
morning, and is still singing beautifully. Well, dear
Mum, please give my love to Daphne.

God bless you. I am your loving First-born son,
CHRISTOPHER TENNANT.

P.S.—When you come for the Sports I shall have
to call you "Mother."

October, 1907.

There is a probable match on the 20th of this month
against a school near here called Winton House. The
watch you sent me keeps perfect time. In the morn-
ings, when we are dressed, we learn one verse. I have
learned the 46th Psalm, and am learning the 30th. We
say our verses to the prefects.

It is a very cold day to-day, and raining hard. The
wind is howling through the trees, and I cannot describe its force. . . . I hope that "Daphne is quite well
and sleeps well and enjoys her food." [2] I am fourth in
my class, and hope to get on well in this school. The
German servant Carl has gone yesterday (to be a soldier) back to Germany.

---

[1] An elder boy charged with the duty of showing a new boy the
ropes and generally befriending him.
[2] The formula used by his old nurse to signify "All well," when
writing to his parents when they were abroad. *See* p. 105.

Another of my teeth has come out, which I enclose. . . . I give most hearty love to you, Deedooge, and Daphne.

October, 1908.

I am getting on well with my work. I think of The Darling,[1] and know she is helping me. It was very cold this morning, although the sun was shining. I hope you like Florence. I am doing well in Greek. The boy whom I like best in the school is Browning[2] . . . all the boys in the school are playing with "Diabolo."

June 13th, 1909.

DEAR MUM,—To-day is Mr. Helbert's birthday, and we have just had an enormous cake, with 1909 B.C., which stands for birthday cake; it was in the middle of the hall upon a stand. We all had two big helpings, and even afterwards some small boys came and looked longingly at it. We all tried to guess how old Mr. Helbert was, but he would not tell us then. I myself think he is about 40 or 41. I did very well in the half-term exams., and was second, but in everything, exams. and work during the term, I was TOP! . . .

West Downs, June 20th, 1909.

DEAR MUM,—On Friday the Fire Brigade came up, and the St. Cross dormitory was cut off, and the fire was supposed to have burned the stairs. They had a huge ladder and the firemen climbed up it and rescued us. The ladder was two long ladders joined together,

[1] His only sister, Daphne, who had died in the previous July.
[2] Now a Captain in the Grenadier Guards. Croix de Guerre, 1917, and D.S.O.

and one man turned a handle round and round and it gradually went up. Then the real engine itself came up, and sparks flew in every direction, and they squirted water on to the house. I enjoyed it so much.

Yesterday we had a Paters' match. We made 82, and then they went in and made 67. We went in again and made 66 for no wickets. So we beat them, and afterwards went down the bank and had a picnic; we threw buns and things at each other, but towards the end it began to rain, and we rushed about with hot tea under a sort of awning. I don't know what my prize is going to be, but I think it will be very grand.[1] Winchester and Reading were going in for it, but I was first of them all. I sit top of my class, and am getting on very well. The summer holidays are very near now. Much love.

September 19*th*, 1909.

I am getting on quite well. We are now playing footer, and I play left half. Mr. Rose gave a lecture last night upon aeroplanes, and I am sending you some notes that I made at the time. There are two "sections" of the top class, and I am head of the second. I am also appointed by Mr. Helbert to look after the whole top dormitory when (as often happens) the prefects are out of the room. I like it very much.

God bless The Darling.[2] I am sure Fred[3] and she are often with us both.

[1] The first prize in a competition organised by the "Alliance Française":—Gallia, Comité de Reading, XV. Concours de Français, 1909. Premier Prix en Lecture et Récitation. 19 Juin, 1909. Christopher could speak both French and German readily, through his home training.

[2] Daphne (obiit July 21st, 1908).

[3] F. W. H. Myers (obiit January 17th, 1901).

October 31*st*, 1909.

DEAR MUM,—I am writing to wish you very many happy returns of your birthday. Well, I hope you will have a very happy birthday, Mum, with the dear Darling, God bless her, watching over you and with you.

The time is drawing near when you give away our prizes at the Cadoxton schools. Have you got another of Oliver Lodge's books to read together in the holidays?

I have determined to try and support the Prefects, but I don't seem to quite know how to do it? but there, I will do my best and cannot do more. Well, dear Mum, again wishing you a most EXQUISITE AND JOYFUL BIRTHDAY, and warm and sunny. Let it be "the day that the Lord hath made." Your loving and adoring son,

CHRISTOPHER.

November 21*st*, 1909.

DEAR MUM,—All is well here. This morning Mr. Helbert gave us a New Testament all in Greek; at first I could not find anything at all, but at last I recognised some words. I received during the match an extremely mysterious and interesting-looking telegram! I could not open it in the middle of the match, which I must tell you we won (score: W. D. 3, other S. 2), but I opened it at the end! I could hardly speak with joy!!! When I read the contents! So dear Alexander has arrived![1] Well, I have written to him to tell him how much I love him. We have great things to thank God and The Darling for. Words cannot express my

[1] His brother, born November 20th, 1909.

excitement, but I shall soon see Alexander; may he be indeed Alexander "the Great"!

All is well here. There is no news. Much love. —Your adoring   CRUFFER.

January 29th, 1910.

All is well. The Doctor says my knee is decidedly on the mend, and I think it is nearly well now. . . . Several of the Masters come to see me regularly, and Mr. Helbert comes over and reads to me every day, which I think very kind of him. The real pleasures I enjoy here are the evenings, when I recall fragments of poetry such as "Aye, note that potter's wheel," [1] "O to mount again where erst I haunted, where the old red hills are bird enchanted," [2] Again, "Say not the struggle naught availeth." [3] I simply delight in them; they are companions to me. Well, dear Mum, God bless you.

February 4th, 1910.

DEAR MUM,—I am charmed with the poem of Rossetti's. I should like to know who Rossetti is? He is not a person I *know,* like Browning or Clough. I suppose he is a person like Dante? At any rate, he wrote wonderful poetry. Did he not write "Does the road wind up hill all the way?" [4] I read that poem often. When one has read it once or twice it suddenly dawns upon you, and every time you read it you get more out of it each time. It is so vast! It is more than

---

[1] "Rabbi Ben Ezra," Browning.
"In the Highlands," Stevenson.
Clough.
[4] Christina Rossetti.

simple poetry! I shall be very pleased to have "The old plain men have rosy faces." [1]   Doctor says my knee all right again.   Am just going down to dinner, and shall do lessons as usual.

June 5th, 1910.

To-day the match-cards are given out by the captain of the eleven.   There is a second-eleven match next Saturday.   I am getting on very well with my music, also with my cricket!   Well, dear Mum, I long to be with you.   I often imagine you sitting in the drawing-room with Clytie [2] and the Icon. [3]   The Darling must be often passing between us.

All is well here.

June 19th, 1910.

The sports are drawing near, and I hope to see you on the 23rd.   There will be another "Hesperid" [4] for the sports, of which I am one of the editors.   It goes to be printed early to-morrow morning.   I think it is going to be very good indeed.   I and Tennant minor have written a long account of Mr. Helbert's birthday.   You will see an account of my day there.   At the end of our account we put

"Long live Mr. Helbert!"

but he would not put it in!   The "Hesperid" is, as you know, our school paper.

[1] "In the Highlands," Stevenson.
[2] A cast of the bust in the British Museum.
[3] An ancient Russian icon given to his sister Daphne by her god-father, Dr. Hagberg Wright, brought back by him from Russia, where he had gone to visit Tolstoi at Yasnaya Polyana.
[4] The School Magazine.

The editors are:

> Tennant ma.,[1]
> Tennant mi.,[2]
> Goff [3] assisting,
> Ramsay [4] assisting.

We have each done a lot of it. I think you will like it immensely. I am keeping my reputation up as a prefect, and will do so all through the end of the term.

September 18*th*, 1910.

There is going to be a French play at the end of this term called *Le Bourgeois Gentilhomme*. It is by Molière. You no doubt know it. Tennant minor is acting the part of M. Jourdain, the bourgeois; I am acting the part of Madame Jourdain, who is supposed to be very sensible! The play is frightfully amusing; I roared with laughter as we went through it. There is no news. I am getting on very well indeed.

December 4*th*, 1910.

Yesterday evening the long dormitory acted *Hamlet;* it was very amusing in parts, especially when the ghost came in wrapped in a sheet! But it was nothing compared to *The Taming of the Shrew*.[5] I shall be able to make sure of my French play in the holidays,

---

[1] Himself.
[2] Edward Wyndham Tennant, later Lieut., Grenadier Guards. Killed in action September 22nd, 1916.
[3] T. R. C. Goff, Lieut., Scots Guards. Wounded October 9th, 1917.
[4] W. A. Ramsay, Sec.-Lieut., Oxford and Bucks Light Infantry. Prisoner of War.
[5] In which he had recently acted, taking the part of Petruchio.

as it is definitely postponed to next term. I send you an Order in which I came out head boy, so I am still retaining my position as top of the school.

The Christmas holidays this year were spent at Hubborn, a pleasant old house near Highcliffe which his parents had taken for the winter. It was within easy reach of Christchurch with its fine Priory, of Barton Cliffs famous for their fossils, and of the New Forest, which the family party explored in many directions by motor.

The beauty of the country lying round Burley, Picketts Post, and Lyndhurst was a joy to the boy. More than once he visited Rufus Stone—a memorial marking the spot where William Rufus was slain whilst hunting in the New Forest in 1100. The stone is surrounded by magnificent beech woods, then in all the loveliness of their winter state, bare branch and spray rising from the russet carpet of their fallen leaves.

A small incident recorded at this time in his Mother's diary gives an insight into one side of the boy's nature. He had been promoted during these holidays to joining his parents at dinner on two evenings in the week. This was a welcome change from the "early to bed" régime, precious too as a sign of emancipation from childish things. But after a week or two he suddenly gave it up and reverted to the early supper arrangement. Perfect freedom—in so far as it is compatible with a child's safety and the give-and-take of family life—being the law of his upbringing, the change was accepted by his parents without comment, and it was not until a few weeks later that the cause became known to his Mother, who noted it in her diary as follows:

"Much touched yesterday to find Christopher had voluntarily abandoned his two late dinners a week with us because on the nights he stayed up I did not read the Bible and pray with him as my custom is on other nights. Rather than miss this he went to bed at 7.15 p.m. instead of dining with us. Arranged in consequence that he should stay up once a week, and that I would read to him as usual on that night."

To the end of his days the things which are unseen and eternal remained very real to him. Free from the least trace of priggishness, his attitude to this side of his life was entirely natural and entirely unconventional. He accepted the outward forms of Anglicanism but he never found in them the natural expression of his religious sense. Dogma had no meaning for him, still less the idea of religion seen as a useful kind of police force to restrain the young and adventurous—a view secretly held by many adults. He was on the side of the rebels on this as on many other questions, but it was the rebellion of one lit by an inner vision, who found in the official system little that satisfied his sense of the immensities with which his individual life was hedged.

He did not return to West Downs at the beginning of 1911. During the past term there had been a number of cases of Hoffman's bacillus (a more or less harmless germ often found in the throat) in the school, and the order had gone forth that each boy's throat was to be swabbed before his return from the Christmas holidays. Bacteriological examination showed that the bacillus was present in Christopher's throat, and there was nothing for it but to keep him at home and give him such help with his work as a tutor who came three times a week from Winchester could provide.

He was already keen to try for a scholarship at Eton (which his grandfather had entered in 1841) or at Winchester, and the loss of the regular term's work was a set-back which made the prospects of his getting one rather remote. By the end of March he was passed free from germs and returned to West Downs. Early in April a chance vacancy, due to the ploughing of a candidate, occurred in K house at Winchester College. This was offered to Christopher through Mr. Helbert, and it was decided that he should accept it and try for a scholarship in the following July. He left West Downs in April and went in May, 1911, to Kingsgate House, Winchester (Mr. R. D. Beloe), where he was to remain for the next five years.

SUPPLEMENT TO CHAPTER VII

As an example of the effect of the Great War upon the careers of the boys who were together in a private school in 1909, the following complete list of those who were at West Downs in 1909 is included, the particular war service being noted against each name, at or about the date of August, 1918.

WEST DOWNS

DIVISION LIST

Short Half, 1909 (Winter Term).

IV.a.

ARCHER	Major, R.F.A. and R.F.C., Flight Commander. Military Cross.
PIGOTT	R.F.A., Sec.-Lieut. Killed in action.
SEELY, MA.	Hampshire Regiment, Sec.-Lieut. Killed in action, April, 1917.
BEITH	19th Hussars, Lieut. Wounded.
CRAWLEY	R.B., Sec.-Lieut.
DEANE	Lancashire Fusiliers, Sec.-Lieut. Wounded.

TENNANT, MA. . .	Sec.-Lieut., Welsh Guards. Killed in action, September 3rd, 1917.
DE BURGH	R.F.A. and R.F.C., Capt.
BOSTOCK	R.H.A., Sec.-Lieut.
RAMSAY	Oxford and Bucks Light Infantry, Sec.-Lieut. Prisoner of War.
MORLEY	R.N., Sub.-Lieut.

SINCLAIR	. . . .	R.N., Sub.-Lieut. Invalided out: Woolwich.
MACKESON	. . . .	Rifle Brigade, Sec.-Lieut. Died of wounds, August, 1917.
STEWART	. . . .	Hussars, Sec.-Lieut.
FRENCH	. . . . .	Irish Guards.
BROADHURST	. . .	Gordon Highlanders, Sec.-Lieut. Twice wounded.

IV.b.

BIRKBECK, MA.	. .	Rifle Brigade, Captain. Military Cross.
SELBY-LOWNDES	. .	19th Hussars, Lieut. Wounded.
PALMER, MI.	. . .	R.F.A., Sec.-Lieut. Gassed, June, 1917.
TENNANT, MI.	. .	Grenadier Guards, Lieut. Killed in action, September, 1916.
PASTEUR, MA.	. . .	M.G.C., Captain. Military Cross.
CARTHEW-YORSTOUN		Black Watch, Sec.-Lieut.
COLLINS	. . . . .	R.F.A., Sec.-Lieut.
PALMER, MA.	. . .	Argyle and Sutherland Highlanders, R.F.C., Captain. Wounded.
PURDEY	. . . . .	Argyle and Sutherland Highlanders. Lieut.
BROWNING	. . . .	Grenadier Guards, Captain. Croix de Guerre, D.S.O.
DAVIES	. . . . .	West Yorkshire Regiment, Lieut. Wounded.

III.a.

PHILIPSON-STOW	. .	R.G.A., Sec.-Lieut.
SOMERVILLE		
HEATON-ELLIS	. .	R.N., Sub.-Lieut.
BIRKBECK, MI.	. .	R.F.C., Flight Commander. D.F.C.
GOFF	. . . . . .	Scots Guards, Lieut. Wounded.
COTTON, MA.	. . .	R.N., Midshipman. Killed in action, May, 1916.
WOOD	. . . . .	R.H.A. and R.F.A., Sec.-Lieut. Wounded.

BAINES . . . . .
WALTER . . . . R.N., Sub.-Lieut.
McCORQUODALE . . Sec.-Lieut., Scots Greys.
HAWKER . . . . Sec.-Lieut., R.F.A.
RANDOLPH . . . . R.F.A., Sec.-Lieut.

III.b.

MARTIN-HOLLAND, MA. Lancers, Sec.-Lieut. Killed in action, March 26th, 1918.
ROUQUETTE . . . R.G.A., Sec.-Lieut.
McCONNEL . . . Scots Guards, Lieut.
SMITH, MA. . . . R.N., Sub.-Lieut.
OSWALD . . . . . Bengal Lancers, Sec.-Lieut.
MOLYNEUX, MA. . . Guards, Sec.-Lieut.
GASCOIGNE . . . . Grenadier Guards, Lieut. Died of wounds, April 12th, 1918.
BUCKNALL . . . . Hussars, Sec.-Lieut.
PASTEUR, MI. . . . Sec.-Lieut.
DUTTON . . . .
MILES-BAILEY . . Hampshire Regiment, Sec.-Lieut.
KNOLLYS . . . . Rifle Brigade, Sec.-Lieut. Wounded.

II.a.

HOTHAM . . . . .
WHITE . . . . . .
WILKINSON . . .
SEELY, MI. . . . .
FELLOWES . . . . R.N., Sub.-Lieut.
POORE . . . . .
GRAHAM . . . .
PHILLIPS . . . . R.N., Sub.-Lieut.
MARTIN-HOLLAND, MI.
SHIRLEY . . . . .
TENNANT, MIN. . . R.N., Sub.-Lieut.
VAUGHAN-JOHNSON .

II.b.

LINZEE . . . . . R.N., Midshipman.
MOLYNEUX, MI. . . R.N., Midshipman. Killed in action, May, 1916.

REES	
CHILD	R.N., Midshipman.
MORANT	Artists' Rifles, Private.
PARKER	
PEACOCK	

I.

TYRONE	
BLACKETT	
COLLINGWOOD, MA. .	R.N., Midshipman. Invalided out.
COLLINGWOOD, MI. .	R.N., Midshipman.
COTTON, MI. . . .	
SMITH, MI.	R.N.V.R., Midshipman.

CHAPTER VIII

WINCHESTER

"Therefore if any young man here have embarked his life in pursuit of knowledge, let him go on without doubting or fearing the event; let him not be intimidated by the cheerless beginnings of knowledge, by the darkness from which she springs, by the difficulties which hover around her, by the wretched habitations in which she dwells, by the want and sorrow which sometimes journey in her train; but let him ever follow her as the Angel that guards him, and as the Genius of his life. She will bring him out at last into the light of day, and exhibit him to the world comprehensive in acquirements, fertile in resources, rich in imagination, strong in reasoning, prudent and powerful above his fellows in all the relations and in all the offices of life."

SIDNEY SMITH, quoted by Ruskin, in "Præterita."

In the belief that parents of past and future Winchester boys (or "men," as they are officially called) may be interested in details of life there, this chapter is left longer than it need otherwise be. The letters all exhibit the dominating influence of his Mother, and in some of them he shows himself rather "old" for his age. But that is rather characteristic of serious boys of fourteen, and as they grow in real experience they get younger in expression and probably in feeling. The phase is a necessary one to go through, and we ought to be able to sympathise with earnest young enthusiasm, for it is surely a mistake to inflict on youth the reticences and precautions—miscalled the disillusionment —of age; nor can we expect from youth a premature abandonment of expressions of self-conscious enjoyment.

It may be, after all, that the illusion is on our side: youth may recognise serious values more clearly than we, who have the world too much with us, and, perchance, by getting and spending have laid waste our powers. When we remember all that boys have to go through, we can read their home letters with a sympathetic eye.

AGED 13.

Kingsgate House, Winchester, May 14th, 1911.

DEAR MUM,—All is well here. I am in the Chantry [2] quire, and like it very much. You can imagine me in that beautiful place. I am not allowed to wear my white boots until I am in the first eleven! I have to

[1] Winchester College is one of the oldest and most famous of the great Public Schools of England. It was founded by William of Wykeham (born 1324, consecrated Bishop of Winchester 1367, died 1404) in the fourteenth century. The foundation stone of the Chapel was laid in 1382, and twelve years later the Warden and Scholars entered into possession of the College buildings. The great Outer Gateway was built in 1394, the central niche above it still retaining a beautiful statue of the Virgin. The College has undergone extraordinarily little change considering its five hundred years of existence. There are now 70 Scholars and nearly 380 students, not on the foundation, who reside in Tutor's houses. The motto of the School, given to it by its Founder, is "Manners Makyth Man."

[2] A two-storied building surrounded by cloisters built by Fromond, Steward of the Hants and Wilts estates of the College until 1420. Used now as a chapel for the juniors, who number about one hundred, and must spend at least a year in Chantry before passing into chapel.

know all the colours and cups, etc., and "Domum"!
I am learning hard, but I have got over a week more.
My "Toys" are so delicious, with The Darling and all
my photographs.[1] I have been oiling my bat. My
form master is very nice. Our class-room is a very
nice and large one. There are about 20 boys in my
div.

Generally I get up at 6.15 and dress. Then I go
over with a socius [2] to school, and we have one hour's
lessons (called Morning Lines). Then I come back to
the House *very* hungry and have breakfast. After
breakfast we do anything we like; go down to shops,[3]
etc. Then we come up and work till lunch. We have
lunch, and after lunch we do anything we like. Then
I go down to the nets and watch out (field) or play
crockets.[4] Then I come up and work till tea. After
tea we do anything, and then have toy-time, when we
prepare for the next day; then prayers and then bed.
When the clock strikes ten all talking stops, and I go
to sleep.

A long day!

Kingsgate House, Winchester, May 14th, 1911.

All is well here. I find we never wear our dressing-
gowns except once or twice. When we go to our cold
tub in the morning we simply wrap a towel round us

[1] "Toys" is the Winchester name for the place where each man
keeps his private belongings. *See* p. 135, footnote.
[2] A companion; it being a bad "Notion" to walk into Meads between hours without one.
[3] The shops in College and Kingsgate Streets, which are *licet* for
men in the School.
[4] Cricket.

and go like that! . . . I have been learning "Domum,"
as Notion examination is next Wednesday! You have
to stand in a row in prefis' lib.[1] All men compete who
have not been here two years, so each term for two
years I shall have to know and say my notions.[2] It is
a bad Notion to take a coat and umbrella. You may
only take one! It has been raining this morning. I
took my umbrella to prevent spoiling my cather (top
hat). I have got all my delicious photographs in my
toys. You and the Darling and Deedooge and little
Alexander. . . . I was bottom out of 26 boys at the
beginning of the term. I am now fourth. I hope to
rise to top and then into a higher division. . . . Moberly Library [3] is a magnificent place. It is a *large*
room, full of books. There must be silence. There
are marvellous books all in different headings, Poetry,
Fiction, Classical—you can think of me withdrawing
there and having peace!

May, 1911.

Mr. Rendall has been appointed Head Master. I
like him, and think he will make a very good one. I
have just been to Gunner's hole (the school bathing
place); it is all in the open air and so delightful. We
bathe with nothing on, and it is *very* slow running
water. It is an enormous place and so nice. I can swim
quite a long way now.

---

[1] The sitting-room of the prefects.
[2] Any word, custom, person, or place peculiar to Wykehamists, and
handed on from one generation to another, is called a "notion." *See*
the vocabulary "Winchester College Notions," two vols., 2nd edition,
1910 (Wells, booksellers to the College, Winchester).
[3] The School Library, opened in 1870, and named after a former
Head Master.

My work, only as far as marks go, is not getting on well. The thing that pulls me down in marks is the weekly Essay on Saturday night, and somehow I cannot do them well. But in other respects I am working hard, and as long as I know that it is all right, and you do not have an Essay in Scholarship Exam. I must work doubly hard to catch up in other ways. Pray for me, dear Mum. The Darling is sure to help me, and I hope to get on very well. I am now "in course" for toy-room,[1] which means I have to sweep out toy-room two times a day! and I also have to put changing-room straight. If you do not do this you get beaten. Some men have already been for not sweeping out! I do not think I shall forget!

July 14th, 1911.

All is well. I was cut out from scholarship. Only just over 20 out of 80 were left in. Mr. Helbert said some of the papers were *very* hard. I have got them all. Some were easy. All well.

October 1st, 1911.

Oh! Mum,—I shall soon be 14! I sometimes feel very lonely, and feel there are many things and many people I do not understand. I feel that my life might be more than it is, and that I might be more of a com-

---

[1] The room surrounded by the toys of the men, and in which they do their preparation. Each man has his own "toys," an upright cupboard about 5½ ft. high and 1 ft. deep, in which he keeps his books and other belongings. It is divided into two parts by a slab projecting out at about 30 in. from the floor. The upper part contains three shelves, the top and bottom ones being usually reserved for books and stationery, the middle one for ornaments and photographs. The seat is 18 in. from the floor, and quite separate from the toys.

panion to you and closer to you than I am. I love you so, so very much, and suddenly I realise that all life is so wonderful and I am so small and understand so little of things. The days here seem empty and monotonous. I am very happy, however, and am getting on with the other boys simply splendidly!

I do enjoy my work. I am nearly getting out of the drudgery, and I often feel intense joy in Horace, Xenophon, etc. I am now sitting top of Mid Part II. I worked my way up, but there are some very clever men in the div. God bless you, my darling mother. Oh, if only we two kindred spirits could flee to the haunts of joy and peace—to see "magic casements opening on the foam of perilous seas in fairy lands forlorn"! [1]

I think of Maud Allan [2] unfolding like a lovely flower! Sweet joy is mine now. [3] Mizpah. Your adoring

CRUFF

AGED 14.

October 31*st*, 1911.

DEAREST DARLING MUMSEY,—Many, many happy returns of your birthday. I hope and feel sure there is a very happy year in store for you, and that the Darling will bless you abundantly. You know it says in Proverbs, "Blessed is a virtuous woman, for all her children rise up and call her blessed." All your children do bless you and love you more than words can express. Your dear "buffday" will always bring

---

[1] Keats, "Ode to a Nightingale."
[2] Then dancing Mendelssohn's "Spring Song" in London.
[3] *See* Blake, "Songs of Innocence."

you the thought of an infinite store of happiness for future years. I wish I could be with you to-morrow, but I shall always be thinking of you. I hope you will have a really nice fine day. I remember well when we took X to The Nameless Spot and saw dear Fan Gihirych.[1] Think to yourself

> I happy am,
> Joy is my name.

Sweet joy befall thee![2]

P.S.—I save just been out to tea with Mr. Robinson, my late div. master. After a good tea we all read the "Midsummer Night's Dream," each taking a part. I was very dramatic and Coquelinish![3]

God bless you.—Your adoring   CRUFF.

Early in November of this year Christopher had a severe attack of measles, which affected his heart, and by medical advice he was sent home on sick leave. He did not return to Winchester until the end of the Christmas holidays.

The interval was spent at Hilders, a house which his grandfather, George Pearce-Serocold,[4] had taken for

---

[1] One of the Breconshire mountains. *See also* p. 87.
[2] Blake's "Infant Joy" in "Songs of Innocence."
[3] Coquelin *aîné* was a personal friend of the family.
[4] Obiit July, 1912, aged 84. Leaving Eton in 1841, George Pearce-Serocold joined the Navy, and sailed with the last of Nelson's captains, Sir William Parker, who became Commander-in-Chief of the Fleet in the first China war, and flew his flag on the *Cornwallis*. After the storming and capture of Ching Kiang Foo, the Treaty of Nankin was signed in 1842, George Pearce-Serocold, as the youngest midshipman in the Fleet, carrying the treaty to be signed on a silver salver. He subsequently saw a good deal of active service in H.M.S.

the winter on the slopes high above Haslemere, and not far from Hindhead. The surrounding country—called by Tyndall "the Switzerland of England"—was explored in every direction, and many places of interest further afield were visited more than once. Aldworth, Tennyson's summer home, with the view over the Sussex Weald "long known and lov'd" by the poet,

"Green Sussex fading into blue,
With one grey glimpse of sea,"

was but a few miles away.

The great house at Petworth, which is thrown open to the public on certain days, was also an attraction for the sake of the fine collection of pictures which it contains, examples of Raphael, Titian, Holbein, a grand portrait of Rodney by Sir Joshua Reynolds, and some very beautiful Turners, hung for the most part not in the unattractive bareness of a picture gallery, but set about in rooms which are lived in, and gaining immensely thereby. The run through the park surrounding Cowdray Abbey, near Midhurst, was a favourite motor drive; the great avenues of leafless trees, and the stretches of park land where deer were often to be seen, made the place a veritable winter fairy land.

In another direction lay Newlands Corner, approached by Albury and up a slope dotted with juniper trees. The beauty of the well-known view, with

Waterwitch, then employed in the suppression of the slave trade on the West Coast of Africa. After his retirement from the Navy he spent ten years sheep farming in Queensland, Mount Serocold in Central Queensland being named after him.

the little church of St. Martha in the foreground and
the bold outline of Hindhead in the distance, was an
unceasing delight; on grey days, on days of sunshine
and cloud, by morning light or in the gathering dusk
of a winter afternoon, it was always touched with something of the mystery of perfect loveliness.

The eastern side of Hampshire was also accessible,
and among other places expeditions were made to Sel-
borne, where a beautiful triptych of the Dutch School
glows like a jewel above the altar of the little grey
church, and memories of Gilbert White meet one at
every turn; and to the old town of Petersfield, with its
quaint streets and Norman church.

But most loved by the boy and most often returned
to was Compton, that spot sacred to all who have
drawn inspiration from the life and work of G. F.
Watts.

Watts was much more than a name to the boy. The
delicate intimate little appreciation of the Master written by Frederic Myers and published in his "Fragments of Prose and Poetry" (a book which Christopher
knew from cover to cover), had made Watts a very real
personality to him. There was also a further link
through Myers' poem, "Stanzas on Mr. Watts' Collected Works," which contains an allusion to Watts'
painting "Daphne."

Compton is a typical Surrey village, set beneath the
shelter of the Hog's Back, and surrounded by unbroken
country, part arable, part woodland. There is a peace
and a beauty about it to which many who know and

love the place must often have returned in thought through these dark years of War, and over it all the spirit of the Master seems to brood. Limnerslease, his house, stands close to the picture gallery which he built to contain a representative collection of his works. The gallery is a one-storied building (always fragrant with the faint scent of some aromatic wax used for polishing the wooden floor), and on its walls hang many of Watts's masterpieces—"The Slumber of the Ages," of which the painter wrote, "In this picture the great stretches of time, since the earth ceased to be a formless mass, are represented as a mighty Mother, with Man, the child upon her lap, growing to conscious knowledge of himself and of his place in the scheme of creation;" "Paolo and Francesca," swept along—but together—by the winds of hell as Dante saw them; "Orpheus and Eurydice," and—perhaps the gem of the collection—"Endymion." "As he lies asleep, his staff in his hand, his dog sleeping also at his feet, the moon-goddess comes down to him, and, bending in crescent form above him, places a hand beneath his head and kisses him upon the lips. It is as if the beauty of the night-time had become sentient, and felt and obtained response to love, passionate, yet pure and calm."[1]

Other well-known pictures in the collection are "Good Luck to your Fishing," "Dawn," and the portraits of Josephine Butler, Joachim, and the beautiful Rachel Gurney (Lady Dudley).

[1] "G. F. Watts." By J. E. Phythian.

Many happy hours were spent by Mother and Son in this little gallery, which was within an easy motor drive from Hilders.

Adjoining the gallery is the pottery established during Watts's lifetime, and now carried on by Mrs. Watts. Here many things of beauty are made and may be bought, from large pieces such as fountains, bird-baths, and great terra-cotta jars to hold outdoor shrubs, down to tiny bas-reliefs of *putti*, and angels, and reproductions of Egyptian scarabs.

A winding country lane set with trees leads to the new graveyard of the village, a rising slope of green crowned by the Chapel, that unique treasury of symbolic design "built to the loving memory of all who find rest near its walls, and for the comfort and help of those to whom the sorrow of separation yet remains," and described by Mrs. Watts in her book, "The Word in the Pattern."

The full significance of the little building cannot be understood apart from this loving commentary written by one who was closely associated with its building, and whose own work has done so much to make it what it is—a perfect shrine. "A symbol may well be compared to a magic key. In one hand it is nothing more than a piece of quaintly wrought iron, in another it unlocks a door into a world of enchantment." [1] "As far as is possible . . . every bit of the decoration of this

[1] All the passages here quoted are from Mrs. Watts's book, "The Word in the Pattern." The place made a great impression on the boy and his mother.

chapel, modelled in clay of Surrey, by Compton hands, under unusual conditions—much of the work having been done gratuitously, and all of it with the love that made the work delightful—has something to say, though the patterns can claim to be no more than are the letters of a great word; hieroglyphs, and very inadequate as representations of the possible reach of the underlying thought suggested by them."

The decorated brickwork of the exterior is full of beauty. In the belfry hangs a bell, the gift of Watts, which bears the words, "Be my voice neither feared nor forgotten." "Around the belfry, on the north and south sides runs a frieze of doves holding the olive branch, signs of the presence of the Spirit of God speaking unutterable words of peace to the mourner, of healing after fiery trial, of anointing to the high calling of such as can suffer and be strong, of crowning for the conqueror who can rise above the lower plane of self-pity. To the east and west are wings rising out of the heart of a great seed-husk, which, with the trumpet-shaped capitals of the small columns supporting the belfry roof, are designed to suggest that ultimate word of triumph, 'It is sown in weakness, it is raised in power.' "

The interior of the Chapel glows with colour. The walls are covered with designs executed in *gesso*, with a wealth of symbol and invention which satisfies heart and eye, and are painted in gold and rich colours.

"The encircling groups of winged messengers, al-

GRAVE OF G. F. WATTS AND MEMORIAL
IN THE CLOISTER AT COMPTON

ternately representing the light or the dark side of
things . . . would suggest the earthly conditions in
which the soul of man finds itself. The face of the
angel carrying the symbol of light is seen, but the face
of the angel carrying the symbol of darkness is unseen. . . . The corbels supporting a wealth of child
faces (one of the oldest symbols of the soul) carry the
words, 'The souls of the righteous are in the hand of
God—their hope is full of immortality.' "

Above the altar is a painting finished by Watts in
April, 1904—but three months before his death—"a
smaller and somewhat different version of his picture in
the National Gallery of British Art which he called
'The All-Pervading.' . . . He claimed that by line
and colour, as by chords of music, that which cannot
be spoken in words may be said to the eye and ear of
heart and mind. Here he has used the symbol of the
blue sphere starred with flecks of light, to suggest the
whole vast universe—'the rush of Suns and roll of
Systems,' safe in the lap of the great enfolding figure,
and encompassed by the guiding Hands of Love."

A steep path leads from the Chapel to the higher portion of the graveyard, along which a brick cloister runs.
Immediately before it is the Master's grave, and within the cloister is a memorial bas-relief, a small recum-
bent figure of Watts with panels at head and foot from
his paintings "Destiny" and "The Messenger," and
an inscription beneath, with these words from Ploti-
nus:

> "As one that doeth Truth cometh to the Light,
>   So he living sought Light diligently,
>   And dying could say, Now I see that Great Light.
>   So may man's soul be sure of Vision
> When suddenly she is sure of Light,
>   For this Light is from Him and is He."

It was of Watts that Frederic Myers wrote, "For such a man what we call death is reduced to a mere formality; and by an opening of inner vision the immanent becomes the manifest heaven." [1]

This account of Compton, slight and imperfect as it is, will perhaps enable the reader to understand the profound influence which the place exercised upon Christopher. The memory of it remained with him, and in later days he returned there more than once in the spirit of one who goes on pilgrimage.

January 21*st*, 1912.

All is well here. This morning we had that delightful passage about Hepseba ἐψιβα. I was second in Macaulay, and not many marks behind the first man. Our div. Don commented on the magnificence of my paper. I am going to try and get it back to show you, especially the criticism on Macaulay, which was not too severe, and in which I did not give myself away by any downright invective!!! I enjoy my work here, and hope to be senior and get a prize at the end of the term. I am looking forward to seeing you here one day, "all dipt in Angel instincts," [2] as my Red Book hath it.

[1] "Fragments of Prose and Poetry."
[2] Tennyson, "Princess," vii.

The Darling watches over us, and there is no separation in Love. God bless and keep you, and give you great joy.

Mizpah. I am with you always.

February 18th, 1912.

DEAREST MUM,—Oh, what a delightful time we had! Oh, to think we walked arm and arm in all the places I walk in by my wild lone! It was a treat your coming down. I enjoyed the hot dish we ordered together,[1] it was a million times nicer as we ordered it together. I can picture you now in your sitting-room with fire and bulbs, and you can me in my toys. This week will pass and bring at its close the joy of another meeting. We had that Epistle this morning at 11.0: "And now abideth these three, Faith, Hope, and Love, but the greatest of these is Love." I thought of you as I often think of you, and hope the term may fly quickly and we may have a delightful time together. All is well here. I love you very much.

Your own adoring   CRUFF.

February 21st, 1912.

This afternoon I went to the Cathedral Library, after having previously read your delightfully mounted extract you sent me. I went to Rob, who is a delicious old person, and then we went up into the beautiful long room, and how I enjoyed the marvellous manuscripts! You can't possibly imagine the beauty of them.

There were marvellous illuminations, but the most

[1] An addition to the last meal of the day, which may be ordered to be sent in from the school shop.

wonderful of all by far was the VULGATE manuscript, which I saw and enjoyed very much![1] There were letters that went the length of the page which have symbolical pictures in and along them. There are the most brilliantly beautiful colours imaginable!! I saw one of Elijah, and in the letter was the whole story of his life. Half way down you saw the mantle, and below Elisha, on whom it was falling. There were also lovely rings and sapphires there. I did enjoy it.

May 29th, 1912.

Yesterday was leave out day, and as Beloe went away, three of us got leave to go on the river. We got into three boats with paddles. They were rather wobbly at first, and we went a long way, paddling on each side alternately. We took ices in tins, and books, and we lay in these boats in the shade and ate ices! Most delicious! After that we went out in an ordinary boat for a short way. Then after lunch we went again in the paddle boats, which could have sails, but there was no wind. Then we bathed and had tea. We had quite a nice day, really. I have got to clean some boots this afternoon, as I forgot to shut a window in galleries, and so have not much time. There have been a few cricket matches. The "Wykehamist" is just out, and with a splendid article on Classics and the Average Boy!—Your loving

CHISSIFOR.

July 14th, 1912.

It is awfully hot here. I will apply for "Swiss leave" next week. I am looking forward to seeing the

Dating from the twelfth century.

King to-morrow. We all receive him in Chamber Court, and sing "Domum"[1] and "God save the King." Then we meet him again in the Warden's garden, which is a most lovely place.

We are going to win a cricket cup this year; the final round is not quite finished. I have been cleaning brass buttons a good deal this morning. I went to a lecture the other day on "The Processes of Etching and Engraving." Next week we shall be revising for exams.

AGED 15.   *October* 11*th*, 1912.

I had such a happy birthday! My cake is delicious. I gave it all round. We have just had Notion-Examina., and the prefects let me off easily. (I gave them each a *large* piece of cake!) Will you send me my two golf clubs and the bag, so that I may use them, for I want to play golf, and there is another man in the house who has just begun. . . .

I remember

"Act well thy part,
There all thy duty lies." [2]

Where do these lines come from?

January 23*rd*, 1913.

I had the carriage to myself all the way, and a pleasant journey. I arrived safe and got my books. I send you my holiday task, which I had this morning, and

[1] The Winchester Song, supposed to have been carved on Domum Tree (an elm on St. Catherine's Hill blown down in 1904), by a "man" kept back for the holidays, who there committed suicide.
[2] Pope. The correct version is:—
"Honour and shame from no condition rise;
Act well your part, there all the honour lies."

did well in it. I enclose the paper. It was not very hard. I am in Mr. Platnauer's division. He is very nice, and I like him so much. There are three new men, Yates, Kilburn and Ferguson.[1] I am in the same toys and the same dormitory, but a different and nicer bed. I have to sweep out the hall or toy-room next week. Nice to get it over so early in the term! We get up at 6.45. I think of you walking alone in London. However, we shall be together again soon. *Schlafen Sie wohl.*

February 9th, 1913.

I enjoyed the debate I went to. We all sat in Moberly Library, the President, Mr. Quirk, sitting at a large table. To become a member you pay 1s., and then you can vote. Debate is held every other Monday. I send you the rules of the society and a paper which is given to every member of the society.

This is Cathers Sunday,[2] and so I am going again to the Cathedral. I do enjoy the Cathedral, especially the sixpenny parts,[3] and it is always interesting and beautiful. . . . To-day I have finished all my fagging for good, except cleaning boots every day! I am in the middle of "Barnaby Rudge." So delightful!

March 1st, 1913.

Everything goes on much the same as usual here. There is a junior steeplechase soon. There are also athletics (sports) on March 25th. There was an interesting lecture last week on lifeboats by Captain

[1] Killed, 1917.
[2] A separate service is held for the School, in the Cathedral, on the second Sunday of each month.
[3] This fee is charged for admission to the eastern aisles and chapels.

Bathurst. We had a debate in my dormitory on Woman Suffrage. I was proposer; I spoke in favour of it, and the motion was easily carried!

March 30th, 1913.

All is well here. I got a beautiful *driver* (price 5s. 6d.), and I am going to use it to-morrow when I play golf. I was fifth in my block (out of about fifty) in mathematics, and first in geometry. The prize is only given for the whole thing; it was won by a Scholar. I have been reading the "Ancient Sage" and the "Passing of Arthur." They are marvellously beautiful poems! It was so exciting about Monte[1] and the Burglar. Monte found him in a cupboard; he was hiding, and Monte in his pyjamas collared him. The burglar said, "I won't struggle." Monte said, "I don't care if you do!"

How wonderful St. Luke i. and ii. are! I have been reading them. I am truly sorry to lose Nurse, and I do not think we can realise how much we shall miss her. I hope she will come back to us and see us again, and perhaps be nurse to my children!

There are only two more days, and next half will be nice, as I shall have no fagging. To-night we read "Locksley Hall." It is a very realistic poem, but difficult to understand.

Fisher's Hill, Woking, April 1913.

I arrived at Woking and saw Mr. Balfour and Aunt Betty[2] starting off for London. Then I went in the car

[1] Mr. Montague Rendall, Head Master.
[2] The name by which he always called Lady Betty Balfour, though there was no tie between them other than that of close friendship.

to various places to do some shopping, and then I came on here. After lunch I went out with Eve, who is well and in very good spirits. We explored everywhere, and we made a large bonfire. We then got some bread and butter, some butter and some potatoes (raw), and we cooked the potatoes in the embers, and had a delicious meal . . . in the woods. I have been playing the pianola here, which works by clockwork, but you pedal to make the sound. Ruth has got a motor-bike on which she is going to Crabbet to-morrow. I rode it up and down the drive; it is just like an ordinary bike, except that it carries you along! . . .

It seems so strange to be here without you! I wish you were here too. The place is as it was last year. I am enjoying myself immensely. I expect the play will come off well. Eve is the Emperor, and Anthony the hero! I have to drink poisoned *coffee* (instead of poisoned wine, as was previously arranged). Mrs. Sidgwick is here. She is happy and cheerful. Beloe[1] said my report was excellent. I did not get my remove, as there were only five, but I was first in my division for both maths. and French. Beloe's parting words to me were, "I am very pleased with you. You have done well."

P.S.—Mum!! Telegram just arrived.[2] God bless Augustus Henry. We are all so delighted. I am so pleased he has arrived. Your *four* children! I am wildly excited. Love to all.

[1] His first House Master.
[2] Announcing the birth of his youngest brother, afterwards known in the family as "The Wise One."

July 20th, 1913.

DEAR MUM,—In the combined term order I am first. This means first in *everything* except exams. (which begin to-morrow), and I shall be first altogether if I do well in them! I am revising hard, so that I may do well, as exams. count a good deal. I have been reading Lamb's "Essays of Elia"; some of them are very amusing.

The table I am making is practically finished, and looks superb. Monte came into carpenter's shop the other day and admired it and turned it upside down to examine it all over. Well, dear Mum, you are constantly in my thoughts. Much love from your loving

CRUFF.

Chamounix, August 30th, 1913.

DEAR MOTHER,—These are a few Alpine flowers I gathered for you at the Mer de Glace. I hope most of them will be alive when they reach you. There was a thunderstorm yesterday over Mont Blanc, the lightning flashing down upon it, and there was lightning in the sky too, in another place, most vivid flashes lighting up the sky. It is a wonderful sight! I walked on the Mer de Glace yesterday; it was just like a sea suddenly frozen, and is quite solid to walk upon, but occasionally you hear it creaking. The mountains are wonderful, and I feel their power when I see them. I appreciate their character so immensely. Everything is so delightful here, and the people are so intelligent. Love to my Brothers! Your loving

CRUFF.

AGED 16. *October 12th*, 1913.

MY VERY DEAR MOTHER,—Thank you so much for the 10s. you sent me. I should like to choose something with you when we meet on December 1st. I feel a great responsibility when I realise I am 16, and I hope I shall be able to do my best in my work, of whatever sort it may be.

I felt that you were especially near me on my birthday, and I am glad each birthday when I think as I grow up I can be more and more of a companion to you. The outward routine of life seems so trivial, yet it is serious in itself, but I think it is hard to use one's opportunities well. Well, dear Mother, the days are passing, one just like the other, except that I progress steadily in my work. But life is well worth the struggle. You know the line of "Ulysses":

"To strive, to seek, to find, and not to yield!"

I feel that I am helped by those I love, whether near or far. My beloved mother, to you above all are due my gratitude and love.—Your loving firstborn,

CHRISTOPHER.

October 26th, 1913.

All is well here. Winter is coming on fast, and the weather has turned cold. I rejoice in my new warm vests! I am trying to enjoy my time here, and I think I succeed to a large extent.

I have been appointed to the post of Junior Librarian; that is, I suggest, discuss, and am consulted about the new books that are now being got for House Library. Everybody pays 1s. a term to the Library, so we have enough money to buy quite a lot of books a year.

November 4th, 1913.

DEAREST MOTHER,—In the debate next Monday I am going to speak.[1] The motion is, "That this House approves of vivisection," and I speak in favour of the motion; that is, for vivisection. It is difficult to defend, because people will say it is cruel, but could you send me some points or facts about it, serious or humorous, that would help me?

All is well here. I expect to finish the bookcase this term; it is progressing favourably. I am well and happy, and my exam. is to-morrow, and on Saturday we have "viva voce" up to Monte!

Much love, dear mother.—Your affectionate

CRUFF.

November 12th, 1913.

My speech was quite a success, though one or two of my points had been mentioned. I had plenty to say, and though I felt nervous I got on all right, and heard that my speech was good! Each speaker goes up to a large round table at which the President and Vice-President and Treasurer are seated. Paget is Vice-President, and spoke well. The motion was carried by eight votes. I hope I convinced eight people! No *good* speeches were made against it.

[1] At the Debating Society, open to men in Sixth Book and Senior Part.

To his Brother.

November 19*th*, 1913.

My dear Alexander,—To-morrow is your birth-day, and I am sending you a present which I do not expect you have yet received. May you have a happy birthday! Four years is a long time, a great age com-pared with dear Wise One, to whom give my love.

Yesterday I bicycled to Southampton, and we got into a small steamer, and it rolled very much, and we went for a short sail; then we bicycled back in the dark without lamps! Southampton is twelve miles away, and Beloe went with us, and we lunched in a wood.

Give my love to dear Nannie. God bless you on your fifth birthday, and I feel sure you are happy. Much love from your own Big Brer,

Chissifor.

December 7*th*, 1913.

Dear Mother,—All well here. Exams. start next Saturday. I am getting on well here and enjoying my-self, but it is an effort to work hard and get up in the morning! I had a book to read during the term, a term task, and I have the exam. on it on Tuesday; it is Kingsley's "Hypatia,"—quite amusing, but it almost spoils a book to have to work at it carefully. There was an amusing debate the other day on, "Are we bet-ter than our fathers?" The motion was lost by six votes, but I voted for it! I "get up by candle-light"[1] now, but after next Thursday there is no work before breakfast!

[1] Stevenson, "Bed in Summer," in "Child's Garden of Verse."

I have been asked by one of the Dons to "rub brasses" next holidays, which consists of getting a print of some brass figures on church walls and floors by rubbing with heelball on kitchen paper put over them; and there are one or two quite close to Brighton which he wants me to do, and in the summer we may have an exhibition of them here! Knights in armour and other figures in brass can be rubbed, so as to get the imprint of them. All is well here. I am working hard and I hope it may not be in vain!

December 21*st*, 1913.

I shall be with you on Tuesday. How nice it is that all work for the term is over! I have done quite well in exams., being first in both the Greek papers (Euripides and Demosthenes) with some ease, and second in Gibbon's "History," and quite high in the Latin papers, so with luck I ought to get a remove.

The Christmas holidays this year were spent at Brighton, where his parents had taken a house for the winter. The strange beauty of the Downs—so unlike their own Glamorganshire country—appealed strongly to the family party, and long expeditions by motor were made in every direction. Near home, the little church of Rottingdean with its lovely Burne-Jones windows became a favourite haunt, and happy but laborious days were spent in obtaining "rubbings" for the forthcoming exhibition of church brasses to be held at Winchester. New Shoreham, Goring, and the Fitzalan Chapel at Arundel Castle, where no less than six rubbings were made in one day, yielded fine examples of early brass work, the rubber becoming more and more expert as time went on.

January 22nd, 1914.

DEAREST MOTHER,—Your letter, which arrived this morning, was a great comfort to me. There is one new man, and I am in the same bed and toys. Monro is Scotch, a good scholar and teacher. I like him and have been getting on well with him, and my work is interesting. The Bin[1] was raptured with our rubbings, and insisted on opening them. He said they were *very* good. He also tells me that though none of the rubbings have yet been mounted, he himself, aided by rubbers, has determined to cut out and mount on canvas all the rubbings for the Exhibition, as he says they look very much nicer. He showed me some other rubbings, and the best one of all was a *very* black one done near here, but ours are a good deal better than most. The Bin says we can have the rubbings back; how nice they will look in the billiard room!—Your loving

CRUFF.

March 22nd, 1914.

DEAR MOTHER,—All is well here, but there is no news to tell you. I am well and happy and look forward to the end of the term very much. I read this morning, in Mob. Lib., Fred's essay on Virgil.[2] We have read it together, and I enjoyed it very much; it is so wonderful. I am sorry to see ominous preparations going on about Ulster. I hope there will not be a war. How is it that it is so fascinating and so

[1] Mr. Robinson.
[2] Frederic Myers, "Classical Essays."

enjoyable to read about war in things like Homer and Virgil, and yet war itself is really so terrible! Give my love to Alexander and the noble Wise One. As Juvenal says, *Maxima debetur puero reverentia!* Good night, dear mother.—Your loving

CRUFF.

Cambridge, April 28th, 1914.

DEAREST MOTHER,—It was sad to have to part from you this morning, and I do miss you so much. This afternoon I went to Ely [1] and saw the Cathedral, which I much enjoyed, but they were tuning the organ most of the time, which was rather tiresome. I went up the octagonal tower and saw the towers of King's in the distance. . . . I am still doing jigsaws; they distract the mind from anything else. I long to be at Cambridge; Winchester seems dull and monotonous compared with it. Everything is so delightful here. I have had such a happy holiday that it makes it hard for me going back. I am so lonely without you.— Your loving

CRUFF.

Winchester, May 14th, 1914.

This afternoon Gustave Hamel, a famous aviator, came here to fly, and most of the school went to see him. I went, and was much excited to see him rise up, and especially "loop the loop"; that is, turn upside down in the air and let the aeroplane dive right down, and then it rights itself. It was most exciting, and he played all sorts of tricks in the air.

[1] His great-great-grandfather, Dr. Pearce, was Dean of Ely in 1797. He was also Master of the Temple and Master of Jesus College, Cambridge.

I had a long talk yesterday about my work with Monro (I told him I was Fred's[1] nephew, which interested him). He says it is most important I should get my remove this term, as in the next division I should get personal supervision and be under a really fine scholar. It is most important I should do this, as I have only eighteen months till the scholarship.[2] He thinks I have a good chance for it if I work, so I must do my utmost to get a remove into Mr. Carter's division. We chiefly talked about technicalities in my work. *How* hard it is to work well in hot weather!

Your Suffrage work interests me always. I find how people confuse any Suffragist opinion with militancy. I had a long talk with our butler (Witty) on the subject. He thinks it would be all right if propertied women had a vote, but he "doesn't want to see women in Parliament," which, he thinks, would be the swift outcome of Suffrage. Also, a boy tells me Suffrage in Australia is quite a failure. I said I believed it was otherwise! How terrible this liner disaster must be for the relations and friends of those who perished! I am now reading "John Bull's other Island" for the third time; it is most delightful.

To his Grandmother, Mrs. Tennant

Winchester, May 20th, 1914.

Dearest Grandmama,—Your delightful and refreshing letter reached me this morning; all you say interests me.

---

[1] Frederic Myers.
[2] He had decided to try for a scholarship at Trinity College, Cambridge.

Yes; I think, though one has periods of great happiness, life is a struggle, and we climb one mountain only to find another in front of us. Perhaps you know those comforting lines of Clough:

"Say not the struggle nought availeth,
The labour and the wounds are vain. . . ."

People often say, "Oh, you have your life in front of you"; but I feel it is a responsibility to make the best of it. There must be some satisfaction in having most of one's life behind one.

I have not written any poetry lately—one cannot sit down and compose it laboriously—it must come by inspiration. The power to *think*, and to think well, is a rare gift; many people seem very callous and indifferent to the *intellectual* things of life. However,

"If they appear untouched by solemn thought,
Their nature is not therefore less divine."

And what a lot of delightful people there are in the world! It is a great gift to be able to see the best in people—there always is a best!

I am hard at work here, and do not find much time for reading novels. I have been reading a play of Bernard Shaw's lately—I think he is always so delightful, and I am very fond of his excellent plays. I have been playing cricket a good deal lately—I really enjoy it now.

To-morrow being Ascension Day, we get a whole holiday, which is something to look forward to.

Canon Henson, who used to be at St. Margaret's, is coming to preach here this term—he is the finest preacher I have ever heard.

Well, I must say good-bye now; it will be most delightful to see you all on June 2nd. I always enjoy my day in London tremendously.

Good-night, and God bless you.—Ever your loving friend,[1]

CHRISTOPHER TENNANT.

June 7th, 1914.

DEAREST MOTHER,—So glad my bike has arrived. I shall enjoy unpacking it myself when I arrive. Your Suffrage work must be tryingly difficult in some ways —canvassing and the like—but you will look back to it with intense pride when the Suffrage Movement has achieved its object. No doubt, in your work, as in mine, there is a great deal that is enjoyable.

I have only been twice to Cathers since I have been back, but next holiday I am free, I have been intending to go and hear the anthem at 4 o'clock. I have been playing cricket so much lately, but I hope to go next week; another boy advised me and said he had been; the same who is under the delusion about Australian Suffrage [having been a failure]. He is a prefect!!! . . .

God bless you, dear mother, we must each

"Lay his uphill shoulder to the wheel."

I am progressing every day.—Your loving

CRUFF.

Lionel Ford, Head Master of Harrow, preached to-day—a good sermon.

[1] This designation was adopted as the result of a suggestion by his grandmother, who felt the intellectual link between them an even stronger tie than that of blood relationship.

I am now reading "John Bull's Other Island" for the third time; it is most delightful.

June 28th, 1914.

DEAREST MOTHER,—It has been such a joy having Deedooge[1] here for the last two days. We had a most delightful time together, and we both enjoyed ourselves tremendously. I showed him the places of interest in the College and the Exhibition of Brasses, which was a great success. Mine were beautiful! We also watched the match against Eton, which was really most exciting, and ended in a draw; there was not time to finish the match, but if there had been we should probably have won! However, you cannot tell, and the result was considered a draw not especially in either's favour. There were thousands of people here for the Eton match, as nearly everybody had some friends down, and we had brilliant weather; we get whole holidays those two days—very delightful.

Farewell, dear mother. I hope you are getting on well with your Suffrage work. On Eton match day I saw a girl with your colours selling "The Common Cause" [2] here. I was overjoyed, and said to her, "I am delighted to see you here." The first appearance of Suffrage in Winchester!—Your loving   CRUFF.

Llandrindod Wells, July 30th, 1914.

I arrived here safely yesterday, and am very happy with Gaggi.[3] It was a triumph getting my remove—

[1] Childish nickname for his Father.
[2] The weekly paper issued by the National Union of Women's Suffrage Societies.
[3] His maternal grandmother.

such a reward for my work, and makes all my labour worth while! I was in great suspense until I knew I was all right. I am in the Lower Sixth now—I shall be under a Mr. Carter, a great classical scholar, who adores classics and makes his pupils work hard.

We are going this afternoon to Elan Valley waterworks, and I look forward to my run back in the car to Cadoxton on Wednesday. . . . This is a lovely place, and I am enjoying myself.

Winchester, September 18th, 1914.

DEAREST MOTHER,—I have passed my Certificate (by which I am exempt from Little-Go) and the extra subjects for Cambridge, having taken extra mathematics and Scripture included in my certificate. Now, therefore, I can devote more time to classics. I like Mr. Carter; he is very interesting; but the work is hard—not too hard. I shall be doing Greek iambics, Greek prose, and Latin prose or verse all in a week. In my division we do only one Greek book at a time; we are doing the *Antigone* of Sophocles. I have only time to say how much I miss you, and how every year I do feel that you are with me in the spirit—distance cannot separate this.

Farewell, dearest.—Your loving

CRUFF.

October 25th, 1914.

The terrible war seems to be dragging on. Hilaire Belloc lectured here last week, and he said *everything* depended upon the result of the battle on the Vistula. Also he thought there was going to be a big smash-up soon. I am getting on in my work; we are getting through the *Antigone;* it is very fine. I also do Plato and Herodotus "unseen." I did so enjoy seeing you at Fisher's Hill. I went out to tea to-day with May Carter, the sister of my master, Frank Carter, and had a very pleasant time there. They have a very nice house the other side of the Cathedral, with a lovely view from it.

June 5th, 1915.

DEAREST MOTHER,—I hope all is well with you; I have not much news to tell you, except to suggest a plan which occurred to me. It is now drawing near the time of my examination, which is in November, and I suggest I should leave Winchester at the end of this term (which I should not be very sorry to do), and that I should have a month or so's coaching for my scholarship, which would give me more chance of getting one—I do not know if I am doing the right sort of work here for it. Then my exam. would be in November, and I could spend the time before I actually go to Trinity with you, instead of being here at Winchester. I shall soon be 18, and I do not think I should much miss being here. You know, mother, we see so very little of each other as things are, and there are lots of things we could do together, if we had time. —Ever your loving

CRUFF.

AGED 17.

To show that the daily round was not all *couleur de rose,* and to give a faithful picture of life in his House, some indication of other sides ought to be given—sides which often trouble parents, though in deference to ancient custom they try to make light of them. Accordingly the following extracts from three letters written early in June, 1915, by Christopher to his Mother are here quoted:

"I entirely agree with what you say; I think it is best that I should stick on here for the present, though I am not very happy here, and often feel very lonely—there is no sort of intellectual companionship with the boys in my house, who for the most part dislike and despise those who care for such things. . . . I assure you my life here is not a happy one, but I know things will be better next term, and I do not despair; but I only tell you this because you know what a relief it is to tell one's sorrow to anyone who will sympathise. . . . I do not say I have no friends. They are rather acquaintances and no more. You can imagine a large number of boys who loathe work, and who when massed together become somewhat animal-like. It is the loneliness I have been in that has brought me into disfavour, especially as there are a large number of rough boys. They have for the most part some virtues, but are rough, and readily resort to measures of violence. These measures would be more correctly described as one or two incidents by which some who are not my friends showed their spitefulness. It will perhaps help if I tell you that this is a very rowdy house at present. Bullying has always gone on to some degree (not of me), as in all Public Schools. I have not said anything at all to annoy, but I have always kept more or less myself to myself. I have thrown my whole keenness into my work. The prefects are as follows: three mediocre and impartial, one rowdy and hostile (only mentally), and one who is unutterably weak and has no authority. The upper part of the house (just below the prefects) can do more or less what they like without interference from prefects, who probably know that these upper boys hold me in disfavour. I mean that they do not persecute me, but as a rule ignore me. This I like. I am a good deal alone, and then I am happy. . . . I will only add that I do not know nor can I find out who has committed these acts of hostility—trifles in themselves some of them. I will illustrate: I do not know who threw my books on the floor and poured my own ink and brilliantine and glue on them: who tore in half a new tie I had not yet worn, who broke the glass of my picture frames, who broke up a wooden stand for writing-paper I had, who smeared my hair-brushes, one pair with ink, another with leather polish. Nor do I know who poured coloured inks on to my best white tennis shoes, who poured nasty smelling chemicals into my cushion so that it had to be thrown away, who removed my electric globe so that I have to use candles, who broke the front magnifying glass of my gold watch. Such things may seem but trifles and would be ludicrous if they were not very tiresome. If I am a prefect next term, which is very probable, I shall at least have comfort and peace. As it is, no one affects my work: I prepare it in Mob. Lib.,[1] and so do no work in my house except preparation in the evening. I have told you everything. I do not think many boys confide school trou-

[1] The School Library.

bles to their mothers, but I am glad I have done so to you, as *you*, I know, would always understand."

A letter from his House Master, Mr. A. E. Wilson, written in June, 1915, in answer to a letter from Christopher's Mother (it need hardly be said that the boy remained in complete ignorance both of her letter and of the reply) shows that he was fully aware of the facts of the case, and that he sympathised warmly with the boy, although he did not "conform to type": indeed, he took strong measures to stop the trouble.

Writing with full sympathy and understanding, he admits that "the general tone of the House is emphatically not intellectual. . . . I have a set of big men who are pure Philistines, with whom Christopher would never get on, and who are incapable of making allowance for a person of Christopher's temperament and tastes. Most of them are leaving this term, and I think Christopher will be happier next term. It would be a very great pity for him to leave now. He is doing very good work and making most satisfactory progress, and his Division Master, Mr. Carter, is very pleased with him. I wish I could write in a more comforting way about him; but it is better to be quite frank as to what I think."

It should be noted that the relation between Christopher and his House Master had always been and remained to the end an entirely friendly one. That the older man understood and appreciated the boy is shown by the following extract from a letter written by him to Christopher's mother on hearing of her son's death in action:—

"Christopher was such an attractive personality, and I am sure I can fully endorse what Lord Harlech wrote—that we can ill afford to lose such young men as he now. He was always an influence for good wherever he was, and had such a sane outlook that one had hoped for a distinguished career for him."

June 22nd, 1915.

I was very sorry to part from you this morning, but we have had such a delicious time together; I am so glad you came, and you managed to get a lot in in two days. I look forward to your coming down here again: your visit has made everything so much brighter for me, and all the places round about have sweet memories of our happy time together. I hope you arrived safely at Cadoxton, and caught your train comfortably. I spent the afternoon with Gilbert Murray in Mob. Lib., and finished the book. . . . It was delicious your being here, and a very good idea of yours to come. I'm so glad you are on the Executive;[1] it is splendid.—Farewell, dear mother.

June 27th, 1915.

All well here. I talked to Frank Carter yesterday about my scholarship; he thinks I have got quite a good chance. He said that examinations always depended on various things, such as whether one is on one's day at the time, and also on the examiners. He said that when he used to be a master at St. Paul's

[1] His mother had been recently elected to the Executive of the National Union of Women's Suffrage Societies.

he used to send up a good many people to Trinity for scholarships, and he never knew of any case in which the examiners had made a mistake—they never failed to take the good and reject bad people. He said that was owing to the fact that Trinity had a large number of Fellows, and that the papers were looked over by at least three different examiners to get the fairest results. He also said that I was up to the standard of scholarship, and that I ought to have some coaching in the holidays, but that it would not be easy to find anyone. I also talked to Monro about it, and he said that it would be difficult to get coaching in the holidays. He (Monro) said I could try for the scholarship again in March if I failed in November, and that I could try again as often as I liked, after I had gone up to Cambridge.

Llandrindod Wells, July 29th, 1915.

DEAREST MOTHER,—You will have heard from C.C.T. about my remove into the top division. I am now in the first twenty of the whole School. Also that I am going to be a Prefect next term. Carter has told me what he advises me to do in the holidays; he said I must not do too much work. I have got the books with me; the work he advised is to read Homer's Odyssey without looking up the words, but read it straight through like a novel, and that after I had read a thousand lines or so it would be just like reading Shakespeare. . . . I am enjoying myself here; the air is most refreshing. It is a great relief to get out of Winchester after having been there so long, and to be able to take a good rest.

Ever your loving CRUFF.

Winchester, September 23rd, 1915.

All is well here. I am working at nothing but classics, except for two hours' history a week—which I cannot avoid.

I have become a member of the Shakespeare Society at the President's invitation. The President is Monte[1] himself, and the Society is called S.R.O.G.U.S. The letters mean Shakespeare Reading, etc., Society, and we go and read a play of Shakespeare's, each taking a part and reading it. This will be very exciting, and it is such a nice way to read Shakespeare. It is still quite warm weather here. I do most of my work with Monte and Rackam, and some with M. du Pontet. I have only played one game of football since I got back. The house is very peaceful, and everything is running smoothly.

AGED 18. *October 10th, 1915.*[2]

DEAREST MOTHER,—Thank you so much for the beautiful Japanese print you sent me. I have put it up in my toys, and it looks beautiful there; many people to whom I have shown it admired it very much and were surprised at it. I like the sea and those delicious hills. It is quite a joy for ever to me, and gives me pleasure whenever I look at it. . . .

It seems strange to me to be 18! I remember a birthday so well at Cadoxton I had when I was 8, and it seems quite a short time ago. All well here. We had our Shakespeare reading last night. We read the *Merry Wives of Windsor*, and I was "Slender." Monte said to me that I read very well! We all enjoyed it so

[1] The Head Master.
[2] His eighteenth birthday.

much. I talked to Duff about Cambridge. Farewell.
—Ever your loving

CRUFF.

October 30*th*, 1915.

DEAREST MOTHER,—I am writing to wish you many happy returns of your birthday. I send you a little lacquer tray which I got here; it may be useful to you, and I think it is old.

All well here. I am going on Monday, leave-out day, home with Wallop to Hurstbourne, where I shall meet Lord Portsmouth.[1] I shall be very happy to spend Christmas at Cadoxton. I go up to Cambridge on December 6th, and stay there till December 11th— just that week. I am getting on well here, and am very happy and enjoying myself—we prefects are all very united. We have fires every day now, all the day long, in the Prefects' library: it is much easier to work when warm and comfortable—in spite of X.'s maintaining the exact opposite of this! Well, dearest Mother, God bless you, and farewell: I hope you will have a happy birthday.—Ever your loving

CRUFF.

November 21*st*, 1915.

The time of my exam. is drawing near now, and on December 6th I go to Cambridge; I do not know exactly what I shall do when I get there, but I suppose Ernest Harrison will tell me. . . . We had a lecture by a man in the school to the Archæological Society this morning, and I was asked to go, though I do not

[1] A Balliol friend of his father's.

belong to the Society; it was very interesting—about Chinese art. He knows someone at the British Museum, and had got down a crate of ancient Chinese porcelains and bronzes—very beautiful things. Morning lines, the hour we do before breakfast, has changed from 7 to 7.30, and so we get more sleep.

Trinity College, Cambridge, December 6th, 1915.

DEAREST MOTHER,—I arrived here safely this afternoon and found your letter waiting for me: I have got very nice rooms on the ground floor in the Great Court. When I got here I went to see Harrison[1]: he is very pleasant, and told me all I had to do. I have two examinations per day throughout the following week, one between breakfast and lunch and one between lunch and tea. I go back to Winchester on Saturday. It is very dark here at night. It is lovely here: the Great Court looks beautiful, and I have got very nice rooms, a bedroom and a large sitting-room, on the left of the Court as you come in at the main entrance. There is only one other Wykehamist up here, as far as I know, and he is the son of the Trinity organist, so he will be with his father, and I shall not see much of him.

Well, dearest Mother, I hope I shall succeed in the examination; they do not give one too much time for the papers, and I do not go very rapidly, but I will do my best. After dinner this evening I am going to see Harrison again. All well here.—Ever your loving

CRUFF.

[1] Mr. E. Harrison, Tutor of Trinity College. *See* p. 287.

Trinity College, Cambridge, December 7th, 1915.

All well here; I have so far had two papers, Latin verse and Latin translation, one this morning and the other this afternoon. I think I did them all right, but of course I do not know how I compare with others. The people doing the examinations all look very learned!

I had a cup of coffee with Mr. Harrison yesterday evening. He is very nice and cheerful, and has got a great sense of humour; he asked me a lot about Winchester. To-morrow I have two Greek papers, verse and translation. My day is as follows, regularly: I am called at 7.30 by a bedmaker, and breakfast at 8 o'clock. I have a paper from 9 to 11.30 or 12.30, and then lunch at 12.30, and have another paper from 1.30 till 4.30. It is dark at 4.30 now, and the streets have no lights. Then at 7.35 I have dinner in Trinity hall (the same place as I do the examinations in), all the other meals being in my room. I have to order my own meals—which is a problem I have never faced before!

I will write again to-morrow.—Ever your loving
CRUFF.

Trinity College, Cambridge, December 8th, 1915.

I went to Trinity Chapel this morning and copied out the hymn for you, which I send you.[1] I also went to King's Chapel and walked back along the Backs of the Colleges. I hope all is well with you. I have

[1] "When wilt Thou save the People?" by Ebenezer Elliot (1781-1849), a special favourite of his which is included in Trinity College Hymnal. *See also* p. 237.

no news to tell you. My holidays begin on Wednesday, December 22nd.

Of the result of the examination his House Master wrote as follows:—

"Kingsgate House, December 23rd, 1915.
"I am sorry that Christopher has not got an Exhibition at Trinity—he seems to have gone very near it, judging from the letter he received from his tutor. He was apparently up against very stiff competition, for the few Classical Scholarships and Exhibitions which they gave. And he has another chance next year, when I hope he may be successful."

As the result had not been unforeseen, Christopher was not greatly disappointed; on the other hand, he always looked back with satisfaction to the chance which had made him an inmate of the College for those few days. His name is among those of the members of the College who have served in the Army or the Navy during the war. The lists are at present affixed to the screen in the ante-chapel.

Winchester, February 27th, 1916.
I have this time news to tell you—about myself. I am in bed with a sprained ankle, and have to rest it for two or three days, so I am having a good rest, which I enjoy, and there is no pain in the ankle at all. I put it out of joint when tobogganing yesterday—we managed to upset somehow, and my foot was caught by the toboggan and twisted. However, I was able to walk home comfortably, and it was only afterwards

that the joint began to swell and grow stiff. We had a delightful time tobogganing on Hills—there is quite a good run there, and it was a pity I hurt my ankle at the end. We upset because someone got right in our way, and the man who was guiding swerved sharply, and so we slid off. All I have to do is to keep my foot up; it is in a sort of basket which prevents the bed-clothes pressing on it. The snow is deep here and makes everything look many times more lovely. I have got everything I want here—books, etc.

March 2nd, 1916

I have enjoyed this week in bed, and it has given me time for reading. I have read all the Wordsworth and some Bacon, and am now deep in Chaucer. I also read one or two novels in between; to-day I read "Man and Superman" again—it is very delightful and amusing.

Two people in other houses are laid up with broken ankles—not serious, however. Do let us have music at Easter; it is so refreshing, and I often hunger for it during term time, sometimes unconsciously. Last night at about 8 o'clock the electric light got dimmer and dimmer and then went out. We had been warned that this would be an indication of Zeppelins! So in the dark—there was no light anywhere—I groped, or rather hopped, my way along to the Matron. Every-one seemed to be rushing about with candles, but I did not use my bad foot at all, and then we heard there was no Zeppelin alarm, so I went back to bed and in ten minutes the light went on again! There is no news. It is nice having rest and plenty of sleep.

May 4th, 1916.

DEAREST MOTHER,—I have made all necessary arrangements for doing French and mathematics, history and geography, which the necessity of Sandhurst, should it arise, would entail. A good few are in my position and think Sandhurst best. . . . For Sandhurst I have to qualify in English, elementary mathematics, French, history (1588-1901, and "The British Empire"!), geography (main features of the world, and especially colonies), and take also Latin and Greek. The exam. is at the end of June. I have been made a Commoner (or "School" as opposed to "House") Prefect, which is a great extension of power, and a rise for me. I have a Row in Chapel, etc.

I saw Aunt Betty[1] to-day. She was very comforting and glad to find me not depressed about anything. I laid before her my present position with its possibilities.

I should *very much prefer the Welsh Guards* to anything else myself. I am very keen about the Welsh Guards now. I note your letter *re* Lord Harlech, and have written to him and arranged to go on Tuesday. I have got a letter of recommendation from Monte.

Tuesday.

DEAR MOTHER,—When I got to Welsh Guards Headquarters at 11 o'clock they told me Lord Harlech was in Wales and that I could see him at 3.30. I have not seen him yet, but am going to shortly. I went and saw Westminster Abbey and then lunched. I am now sitting in St. James's Park close to the Welsh Guards

[1] Lady Betty Balfour. *See* pp. 149 and 285.

Headquarters, and am going to see Lord Harlech at 3.30.

(*Later.*)

Lord Harlech says I must go to Sandhurst and learn the thing thoroughly. He will give me a letter of recommendation and send it to Winchester.

May 19*th*, 1916.

DEAREST MOTHER,—I have written to you only on business lately, and now that everything is settled I do feel so deeply grateful to you for all you have done about my going into the Welsh Guards. As I have got to be a soldier, that is best. Personally I do not think it will be at all an unpleasant experience—for a few years. My classics may get rusty, and them I shall rub up easily—and I shall never cease to care for the right things—Browning, and the Alps, and all the things we have loved together. . . . The following are the dates of my movements: June 27th, Sandhurst exam. (at Winchester). Beginning of July, leave Winchester for good (this is usual in the case of men going to Sandhurst). First week in August, results of exam. come out. Immediately after, go to Sandhurst. . . . God bless you, dear Mother.—Your loving

CRUFF.

June, 1916.

DEAREST MOTHER,—I look back with great pleasure to our delightful time together. I enjoyed so much having you here, and I think you managed to do a lot of important business in connection with me.

This afternoon I fired at the range and did very

well. Sergeant Bawket said there was nothing in my shooting to worry about, and that I may fire at the range as often as I like, so as to get good by practice. . . . He has been eleven years in the Army, and enjoyed it very much. He was in the trenches nine months, and at Mons with the men who retreated eighteen miles at two miles an hour without any food at all. This eighteen miles was right at the end of the retreat. I think he has taught me a *great* deal, and all of it will be useful to me. . . . Last lesson we went out to a place where there are some real trenches, and he told me all about trench warfare—very interesting.

I shall be sorry in a way to leave here—but not altogether sorry, which is as it should be, I think. Farewell, dear mother. My Sandhurst exam. is coming on soon now.—Ever your loving

CRUFF.

In the second week of July, 1916, Christopher left Winchester for good in order that he might get a short holiday before going to Sandhurst at the end of August.

SUPPLEMENT TO CHAPTER VIII

ROLL OF HONOUR [1]

Of those who were contemporaries of Christopher Tennant's at Kingsgate House, Winchester, the following have laid down their lives in the service of their country during the Great War :—

"K" HOUSE.

T. C. GILLESPIE . .	1905-11 .	K.O.S.B.	1914
A. J. I. DONALD . .	1907-12 .	Manchester Regt. .	1915
A. M. GASELEE . .	1907-12 .	15th Hussars . .	1915
G. R. McGUSTY . .	1907-11 .	Royal Irish Rifles .	1916
R. I. MACKENZIE .	1909-11 .	Black Watch . .	1914
R. S. OSMASTON . .	1909-13 .	Royal Sussex Regt.	1917
E. H. K. SMITHERS .	1909-14 .	Manchester Regt. .	1916
Visct. WEYMOUTH .	1909-12 .	Scots Greys . . .	1915
R. W. ATKIN . . .	1910-15 .	R.H.A.	1917
E. R. HAYWARD . .	1911-15 .	R.F.A.	1916
G. C. S. TENNANT .	1911-16 .	Welsh Guards . .	1917
F. H. HADEN . . .	1911-12 .	Rifle Brigade . .	1917
J. K. FALCONER . .	1911-14 .	Hants Carabiniers	1917
R. NEVILL	1911-15 .	S. Lancs Regt. . .	1918
F. H. PATTEN . .	1912-16 .	R.A.F.	1918
T. H. B. WEBB . .	1912-16 .	Welsh Guards . .	1917
A. NUGENT . . .	1912-17 .	R.A.F.	1918
J. FERGUSON . . .	1913-16 .	R.A.F.	1917
F. A. HICKS . . .	19..-14 .	Royal Fusiliers .	1918

[1] Up to August, 1918.

CHAPTER IX

"Man is the shuttle, to whose winding quest
And passage through these looms
God order'd motion, but ordain'd no rest."
HENRY VAUGHAN (1650).

No excuse seems necessary, at the present time, for giving some idea of life at Sandhurst as seen by a type of boy who has undertaken military life without having been normally in the least attracted by it—a great multitude now.

Royal Military College, Camberley.
August 30th, 1916.

DEAREST MOTHER,—I am going to tell you all my adventures from the beginning. I do not like this place much, but it is not so bad as I expected. I believe it is quite nice after the first six weeks. I left my bicycle at the station and came on here with my luggage in a car with a lot of other men. I first saw the Adjutant, who shook hands and took my name down. Then I came on to K Company. It was a cavalry company before the war. Now Guards and cavalry and infantry are all mixed up. There are about 900 here in all, I believe. When I got here I was shown a room; it is quite a separate room, about the size of the bathroom, and it is nice to have it. Then I saw our sergeant, Sergeant Giles, a fierce-looking man, brawny, with a toothbrush moustache. He took my name and address and gave me my safe key and room number. I also saw the Captain of the Company—he took my name and religion and future regiment! Then I was left alone. It was like one's first day at school. Nobody took any notice of me, and one was a mere cypher. Also the buildings here are like a maze. It is literally impossible to find one's way anywhere at first, and I hardly know the way now. It is like being in barracks here. My room looks on to a square surrounded by other rooms. I found no key to my room. All rooms have a Yale lock on the inside and are supposed to be locked. There was also no plug in the washing basin, so that all the water ran away. I managed to get the key and the plug from my servant after a time. I have got a rifle of my own, and various articles of kit in the shape of belts with water-bottles, etc., on them. We go before mess to an ante-room, which is a sort of large smoking lounge. The new arrivals, or "juniors" (as they are called till the next lot come in, when they become "seniors") are not allowed to go to the upper end of the ante-room, but have to keep down in one corner, and there is an invisible line which one may not cross. If one offends the seniors by so doing, one is liable to be put in an ink bath. All this is very barbarous. The seniors here seem a very rowdy lot. Then we had a good dinner—the food here is very good—and afterwards the senior man of the Company came and talked to the juniors. He gave us a few hints about things. He said "The point of this place is discipline," which about sums it up. The mess-room is dark and ominous, red in colour, hung with military trophies, so different to the majestic beauty of Trinity's hall.

I am lucky in having got into a good set here—the nucleus of which is another old Wykehamist and an old Etonian, called Ralli, a very nice fellow. He, too, was going to Trinity, Cambridge, and was prevented by the war. The course here is about six months. There is no leave till we are "off the square"—that is, finished our drills—which means at the end of a month or six weeks. It depends how we get on, but till then there is no leave. However, we get the following times off, and, I believe, are allowed to go anywhere in those times:—

Wednesday, 2 to mess.
Saturday, 11 to mess.

I believe there is a good hotel at Camberley, if you come down here some time. My time-table is as follows, and very descriptive:—

6.0.	Wakened by servants, who go round with hammers, banging on the doors.
6.30.	Coffee.
6.50.	Drill.
8.0.	Breakfast.
9-1.	Drill. Later other things—riding, etc., or gymnastics.
1.	Lunch.
2-7.	Various military work.
8.	Mess.
9-10.	Sort of "prep." One has to be alone in one's room and look over the book work one has had in the day.
10.30.	Lights out.

We went and got measured this morning and got our gym. things. There are a good many new buildings here. I feel this will get very monotonous after a time, and I shall never like it. Still, I know it is best under the circumstances. I will write again. God bless you. I am with you in the spirit always and feel very home-sick here!—Ever your loving

CRUFF.

We have to pay 2s. a month ante-room subscription. The ante-room is where we go before dinner, and our names are called there. The subscription is to supply furniture, as every single article of furniture, including the piano, was smashed by the last lot of people who went out to take up commissions!

August 31*st*, 1916.

DEAREST MOTHER,—No letter from you yet. All well here. I foresee this place will be quite possible after a bit. I am not at all unhappy, and quite en-joying the time when we are not drilling, as I have luckily got into a good set. This is very fortunate. The people I know here are chiefly old Etonians, and one other old Wykehamist whom I like. I have seen a good many other old Wykehamists about in other com-panies. There are ten companies and about seventy or eighty in each. I have just had a bath (5 p.m.), as it is impossible to get one in the morning. There are only two bathrooms and a few shower baths. The drill is strict, but the unpleasant part of it will be over in a few weeks. We each have a rifle, which we have to keep clean; we have it in our rooms. . . . Some of the seniors are very rowdy, but do not take much notice of us juniors. I am sorry I do not get any leave for the first six weeks, but perhaps I can get over to Fisher's Hill [1] sometimes on Saturdays, when we can go where we like between 11 and 7. This morning we all put on gym. clothes and were inspected in the gymnasium—that is, all the new cadets, about 500 in all. We were inspected by General Stopford, the Commandant. Later we went to a class-room, where the C.O. of our company (Major Tod) spoke to us. He asked us to go to him in any difficulty. I hope all is well with you.—Ever your loving and inwardly unmilitary

CRUFF.

September 1st, 1916.

Could you send me my football boots? I take the *Daily News* every day, and have done so since I have been here. I will certainly try and keep up my classics. I will do the Homer.

We do a good deal of book work, consisting of:

(1) Military Law and Administration.
(2) Tactics (very interesting).
(3) Topography, maps, etc. (all very interesting).

The more I am here the better it seems, and it is all right after one gets into it. I am very pleased about the Prize Cadetship.[2] I get tea daily at 4. It is not supplied, but I have it at a shop or café. I am well and happy. I have got my Madonna [3] up, and my room is

---

[1] The home of the Rt. Hon. G. W. Balfour.
[2] Awarded to him on the result of the entrance examination.
[3] Botticelli's Virgin and Child and St. John (the Louvre).

quite comfortable. . . . I think of you often at Cadoxton. I am going to get "Old Mortality" from the library this evening—you can take books for fourteen days. . . . I am lucky in having the officer in my Company—Senior Cadet—an old Wykehamist: I knew him at Winchester and was in the same form with him.

September 3rd, 1916.

We had church parade this morning and marched to church with a band. This lot of seniors go out in six weeks, and I believe there is a probability of our all getting five or six days' leave then! I hope so. We should then become seniors; this is very lucky, as usually men are juniors for at least three months. We shall be seniors for more than four months. We are doing two hours' drill a day at present. The Adjutant is often there, and he is terribly strict. He drops on you for having your boots laced the wrong way, and that sort of thing! I quite enjoy my leisure time here, it is a great thing having one's own room. . . . It is not so bad as I expected, and, now I have more or less got into it, it is all right, but it may be worse later on. The discipline is very strict, and I do not like that! Also it is a great bore getting up so early. This place is surrounded by a beautiful park, with a lake in it on which men boat. The sergeant who drills us is a nice man, but enormously strict: he expects one to move like lightning, and he is always falling on somebody! One has to keep perfectly still on parade, and some of the rifle exercises are very difficult. One has to make a great deal of noise with the rifle in moving it about. This is quite incorrect from a military point of view, and only done here—so we have to do it! We also have to learn one or two rifle exercises that are done *nowhere else!* This seems such a waste of time. . . . This place is very physically fatiguing, and one gets so little sleep, but I shall only be here seven months at the very outside, and I am sure this is the very best thing that could have happened considering the present circumstances. . . .

September 6th, 1916.

DEAREST MOTHER,—I have written to Lord Harlech. I take in the *Daily News,* the *Saturday Westminster,* and the *New Statesman*—all of which I devour eagerly, as they are a link with intellectual things. I have also got "Old Mortality," but do not enjoy it so much as when we read it together. . . . It seems as though I had been here for months, although the days seem to slip by quickly. It feels to me very strange my being here—and almost like a dream. But it is not nearly so bad as I expected, and though at times one has to do unpleasant things there are advantages which make up for them. We get up at 6 all through the winter! Sometimes I have been so tired that I went to sleep again after being woken, and woke up at 7.25, dressed in ten minutes, and just had time for some coffee. The other night the seniors put two juniors into cold baths and then made them run along passages, beating them with belts and sticks. I do not think I am at all likely to come in for any of this. . . . We breakfast at 9 on Sundays, and may come down at any time. What joy!—Ever yours,

CRUFF.

September 13*th*, 1916.

DEAREST MOTHER,—I send you a very interesting article from the *New Statesman;* I agree with it thoroughly. We spent all this morning digging trenches, in canvas trousers—very hard work. We had to dig ourselves in; each man had a piece of ground 6 ft. by 3 ft., and had to dig 3 ft. deep, throwing the earth up as a parapet in front. We just went out into a wood and marked out trenches and then dug. I had a tree close to my part and had to cut the roots away with an axe. Several trees had to be cut down altogether, as they came in the middle of the trenches. So glad you are reading Ibsen. His plays made a great impression on me when I read them—not so very long ago. I remember *The Lady from the Sea*, well, and *The Wild Duck*, too. *The Doll's House* is very wonderful. Do get those two you suggest, and we could read them together, *The Master Builder* and *Hedda Gabbler*. I have not read them. I do not think I should have time to read the *Welsh Outlook*. All well here. Ever your loving

CRUFF.

September 25*th*, 1916.

DEAREST MOTHER,—I too felt it was terribly hard parting from you yesterday morning—your presence was like a ray of sunshine. I so enjoyed having you here, and it makes it much easier for me, now that you know all about my life here. I heard from Aunt Betty [1] this morning. She asks me to go over to Fisher's Hill. Farrell tells me he has never known anyone hav-

---

[1] Lady Betty Balfour.

ing an extra rough tunic, and that men wear superfines
if they get the others wet. So I am going to wait and
see if it is necessary to get an extra one, and not de-
cide now. I think it would be better to send me the
£3 by post, and not to the Accountant, because people
look in the book and see one has a lot of money with
the Accountant and then press one to lend them money
—if one has two or three pounds there. I got your
letter, written on an envelope, this morning, and it
cheered me up very much. I find two men keep spirit
lamps in their room and make themselves tea sometimes with tabloids.—All well. Ever your loving

CRUFF.

September 28th, 1916.

The seniors have been quite nice to me lately. The
rowdiness has died down. There have been no more
ink baths and not any sort of rowdiness. One of the
juniors told me that the seniors had decided to stop
ink baths for the present.

I am sorry to see Bimbo Tennant killed; I knew him
well—at West Downs, and he was at Winchester too.[1]
When I read his letter I felt it was just the sort of
letter I might have written to you.

October 2nd, 1916.

DEAREST MOTHER,—I am reading "Waverley," and
like it very much. Have you ever read it? It is a
great thing to have something to read in an odd ten
minutes or quarter of an hour. We are finishing our

---

[1] Lieut. the Hon. E. Wyndham Tennant, Grenadier Guards, killed
in action September 22nd, 1916. *See* p. 123. The letter referred to
is one written by him to his mother before going into action.

drill on the square this week, and would have done so last week if the Adjutant had not been ill. I have discovered here a reading room to which any cadet may go any time to read and be quiet. It is in the New Buildings, and I often go there now and read the papers. I even discovered there books by the last person you would expect to find, even Bernard Shaw—and am reading them! Yesterday I went to Winchester with six others—one of them a man who was in my house and a prefect with me. I like him very much and only wish we were in the same company. We got there at two, and Archie [1] gave us some lunch. Then we talked with him and saw the Matron and all the other prefects, etc. It seemed very strange being there, like a dream, and everything so familiar. The atmosphere there was very different to this place. One felt the contrast. We had tea with the prefects, this man and I, while the others went off to their respective houses. Then we went to Chapel and heard the Bishop of Winchester preach, a good and short sermon. Then I had a talk with Monte,[2] who was very refreshing and delightful. We had dinner with Archie, and had decided to meet at the "George" at eight. Archie's clocks were a quarter of an hour late, and we got there to find the others were waiting, and had been for a quarter of an hour, and had sent the car for us—of course we had missed it. By then it was 8.30, and we had to be in by 10.15. The driver said he could do it if nothing happened, and we got on all right till we were about six miles from here. *Then our head-lights suddenly went*

---

[1] Mr. A. E. Wilson, his former House Master.
[2] Mr. Montague Rendall, the Head Master.

out. We were in complete darkness, and could not get the lights to work. We persuaded the man to drive on in the dark, and at a garage hired a small bicycle lamp, which I held. It was ten o'clock, and the others said it was all my fault our being so late. However, our driver behaved splendidly, and we drove on in darkness, our lamp giving hardly any light and being blown out by the wind every minute. The man drove on as fast as he could in the dark; twice we were almost into a telegraph pole, and once we nearly ran into a tree. At last we got to R.M.C., and I thought we were done for. We rushed in to sign our names with the time of arrival. The sergeant called out 10.20! At that moment an officer—the officer in charge—came in, and he was Scotch and very nice. We told him what had happened and he said, "All right, you may put it down 10.15 on the book, not 10.20!" So we were safe and got in in time. The seniors would have made it hot for me if we had been late. As it was, they are so pleased at having got back in time that they do not mind. I so enjoyed going to Winchester. Everybody so nice and pleased to see us.—Ever your loving

CRUFF.

October 3rd, 1916.

I do rejoice in the book[1] which you have sent me. I have begun the Phædo already, and am surprised how easily I can read it. I have got the English on the opposite page to the Greek, and can refer from one to the other when necessary. I find I can read the Greek

[1] Plato, with an English translation by H. N. Fowler. The Loeb Classical Library.

very easily, with occasional references to the English. It *is* a joy to have Plato here, and I shall certainly read daily. I am so fond of Socrates—he seems like an old friend when I come back to him again. It is all so refreshing, and I delight in it so.

This morning I was five minutes late for parade. I never woke up because they tapped very lightly on the doors, so as not to disturb the seniors who had been inoculated the day before, and were to stay in bed this morning. However, I was let off any punishment. The sergeant did not report the matter. I think he is very pleased with me, as I have been trying very hard lately. I do not think my lateness has affected this, but I must not oversleep again! You can think of me reading Plato here; it is a very Xtian way of spending one's leisure time in a military college!

AGED 19.   *October* 10*th*, 1916.

DEAREST MOTHER,—Your birthday letter to me was a great joy—with all the blessings that it brings. It is wonderful to think that I am 19! A year ago I never thought I should be encompassed by all these "military vipers"![1]

A magnificent Etna arrived this morning. It is a lovely one, with handles, and I shall be able to make myself hot tea and coffee. Everything arrived as per list except the bundle of wicks. I read Plato every evening regularly. Deedooge[2] is coming over this afternoon to see the buildings, etc., and I shall take him to my room and show him my rifle and things which you

[1] Some family joke, only.
[2] Childish nickname for his father.

saw. This week we finish our drill on the square and begin Company drill. Everybody says the worst is over when you leave the square.

I look back to all the birthdays I have celebrated, in Cadoxton, at West Downs, and at Winchester—and I think this is the strangest place of all that I have had a birthday in.

> "The old order changeth, yielding place to new,
> And God fulfils Himself in many ways."

I remember my birthday at Cadoxton when I was five, with five candles. It seems very long ago, to me! Farewell, dear mother; I am never completely happy except when you are with me.—Ever your loving firstborn,

CRUFF.

November 1st, 1916.[1]

DEAREST MOTHER,—My thoughts are with you to-day, your birthday. I wish we could have spent it together; I do miss you so much, and I feel it more to-day, sitting alone in my room, than I did yesterday. It is dreadful having to part from you, and everybody.

Coming back to it, I feel the atmosphere of Sandhurst is to me very uncongenial. It makes a difference being a senior, and so on—but it is depressing coming back again, the time seems to go so slowly at first. I have got the same room as before. Three of the seniors have stayed behind, two of them failed to pass out, and the other was caught in London and deprived of his commission. They are in this Company. This

[1] Written after five days' recess, spent at home.

morning we had to get up at six and ride from seven to eight. We only trotted round, and I got on all right. Then we did Swedish drill from nine to ten, and after that two hours' tactics, so I have had an energetic morning. . . .

There is a rumour that our lot will not go out till April; I will let you know if I hear anything definite. I did so enjoy our time together, and every moment of those four days was precious to me. It will be a joy to have you here on the 24th.

I am going to have a sleep now, as I feel tired, so farewell.—Ever your loving

CRUFF.

November 5th, 1916.

DEAREST MOTHER,—All well here; I find life very much easier as a senior, and I get on well with everybody. It was hard in a way to come back here, but now I have got into it again everything seems all right. It is like school in that way.

I was going to see Monseigneur De La Villarmois at Farnborough to-day, but it has been raining all day without stopping, so I gave it up. I spent the afternoon partly with a friend who was at Winchester with me in my house, and partly in the reading room. In the morning I did a little work for an exam. we are going to have next week on "The Infantry in Attack"! I am getting on well with riding: I think I have good hands, and I always feel an affection for the horse I am riding. I am reading in my leisure moments "The Heart of Midlothian." It is very wonderful. I do think it is a help to have something like Scott to live

with and digest—something outside my present sphere
of duties. I am putting my back into all my work
here—much of it is interesting and worth doing well.

I see Oliver Lodge has written a new book, "Raymond, or Life and Death." I saw a review of it in
the *Times* Literary Supplement, and it deals with
topics of an S.P.R. nature.

Our lot do not seem to be very rowdy, except for
the first evening of the new juniors, when they were
exceptionally rowdy, to impress them!!! One senior
dressed up as a junior, and the other seniors mobbed
him. Then an officer came up, and did not recognise
the senior, but thought it was a junior, and he was
very angry!

I so *so* miss you. Farewell.

November 8th, 1916.

DEAREST MOTHER,—Your letter arriving yesterday
was a great joy to me. I do feel thankful that I am
a member of Trinity—that in itself is a great possession for me. As you say, I belong to her, now. Your
suggestion about an article *re* life here is a very good
one, and I will see what I can do—and try to talk
about things that happen here that would perhaps
startle the outside world, though we get used to them
soon enough. . . . This morning we have all been out
with maps, marking in them how we should dispose
outposts and picquets, etc. The country we were dealing with is all flooded, and we had to walk about in
the water! Some men went up to their knees in it, but
I managed to do the work all right without going above
my ankles in water!

It is definite that we shall be kept here till April, unless the rumour *re* Guards going out earlier is true. I do look forward to having you here, dear mother; it seems ages since we were together.—Ever your loving

CRUFF.

December 12*th*, 1916.

I have just won my spurs at riding, which is a great honour, and difficult to do—and now I have got a beautiful new pair of spurs which I shall wear for riding in future! I have written to Lord Harlech. I see the papers every day. What a strange state the political world seems to be in!

January 13*th*, 1917.[1]

All is well: my luggage arrived this morning and I have got it all right. Coming back here has been much less trying than I expected. Now I am here Peter[2] and I and my Irish friends are good company. It was dreadful leaving you; but I enjoyed every moment of those three weeks we had together.

I have got Wells's "Passionate Friends" to read. I went to bed soon after mess. They got us up at six this morning, paraded us at seven for drawing our rifles. That process was over by 7.10, and we had nothing to do till breakfast at eight o'clock! We are having a new time-table now, in which the chief thing is firing at the big range with ball ammunition. There seems to be no more Company Drill. The only things we shall be doing are—

[1] Written after the Christmas recess.
[2] Sec.-Lieut. Peter Harris, Coldstream Guards. *See* p. 108.

Shooting,
Hall of study,
Swedish drill,
Riding,
Digging trenches.

The new lot arrive on the 23rd. I have been over to the Staff College to see our juniors. They are in quite nice big rooms, and they have fires in their rooms, which is very nice for them. I hope all is well with you. You can think of me as happy and untroubled. I miss you all intensely.—Your loving

CRUFF.

January 14th, 1917.

All well here. We had the usual Church Parade this morning. There was a fine rain falling all the time, which later turned to snow. We stood in the rain and were inspected by people in red tabs—I thought of Wells!

Then we had quite a good sermon from the Muscular Christian, who actually quoted "Mr. Britling"[1] to these "military vipers." He spoke of it as *the* book of the day, and quoted that part right at the end where Letty is speaking about God—"a God who struggles, who is akin to Mr. Britling," and how "God is everything that is true, everything that is tender"—you will remember the passage.

January 25th, 1917.

My cold is quite well again now, and I am enjoying life here very much. I made a "possible" at the

[1] "Mr. Britling Sees it Through" had been read aloud during the recess and discussed with his mother until all hours of the night.

range to-day. I got ten bulls'-eyes at 200 yards in rapid fire—*i.e.*, the ten shots have to be got off in forty-five seconds! This is a great achievement! Many thanks for the Wells article. Do send them to me in your letters whenever they come out. How exciting your being an official for next year's Eisteddfod![1] The new juniors are here—some Wykehamists. Five of the juniors fainted on seven o'clock parade this morning. . . .

January 30th, 1917.

Everything is going on well here. We are having glorious skating on the lake. We have finished our course of shooting and I am one of the best shots in the Company. You can be a marksman, a first-class shot, second-class shot, third-class shot—I am a marksman, which is the highest of all. I am also representing the Company in revolver shooting, as I am the third best revolver shot in the Company.

LETTER TO A FRIEND.

Royal Military College, Camberley.

February 13th, 1917.

This is just a line to tell you how much I enjoyed my day with you at Reading. I look back with pleasure to every moment of it, and hope I shall be able to come and see you again.

I also want to tell you my adventures after I left you. The driver took the wrong road, though he asked the way several times, and we went on and on for

---

[1] His mother had been elected Chairman of the Arts and Crafts Committee of the National Eisteddfod for 1918, which was to be held in Neath.

miles, then we stopped to look at a sign-post and found we were going towards Reading! We got into the right road just as the car punctured. So we took the tyre off and went on with no tyre, until the wheel began breaking. Then the driver refused to go any farther, and we were stranded. I discovered we were at a place called Heckfield Heath, near Hook, in Hampshire, with no house for miles round. So I made myself comfortable in the car and went to sleep! I had quite a good night's rest, and was well wrapped up. In the morning the engine was frozen, so we first mended the puncture, and then I had to walk a considerable distance to get some hot water. After that the engine started again, and we got back safely at 9.30 on Sunday morning!

I had an adventurous night of it, and was not at all uncomfortable, and I took everything calmly!

The authorities didn't mind a bit, and were rather amused at my adventures.

February 17*th*, 1917.

We are having a sort of concert to-night. I think juniors are going to sing—voluntarily! If the mumps goes on we may get three weeks' holidays when I pass out, owing to infection. The hospitals are full, and there are mumps quartered in the rooms of A Company!

We were inspected to-day by the D.G.I.C.G.S., which being interpreted is the Deputy General in Command of the General Staff. I had a very wild horse yesterday at riding, he refused to go over the jump and swerved round it, then began kicking, and very nearly kicked old X, who had to jump nimbly aside. Several other officers watching nearly got kicked, and finally the instructor had to get on him and take him over the jump.

I am doing a lot of revolver shooting, as I am in the battalion revolver team—*i.e.*, one of the thirty best shots in the College. The days pass very quickly. I do a good deal of work, and ought to pass out easily. There are really very few subjects to learn up for the exam. when you consider them all. . . . By the way, I read with interest the cuttings you sent me *re* brains in the Army, etc., and also gave them to Harris to read. I hope all goes well with you at Cadoxton. We spend most of our time now doing schemes—going out into the country and putting into practice what we have learnt in theory. There are several cases of measles now, as well as mumps—just developed.

All the skating is over now, and there is very little ice left on the lake. We have finished all our work really, as the course was arranged to last six months, and now they do not know what to do with us, so we are just doing the same old drill most of the time—forming fours, etc.

They have started a clothing inspection now, and we have to put all our clothes out on our beds, then an officer comes round and inspects it. Everything has to be in a particular place, socks with a collar between them, and all that sort of thing!

Our food is also being reduced; we get no sugar now, and all the tea and coffee is sweetened beforehand, and we have our porridge with a very small heap of sugar put on it for us!! You know what a lot of sugar I generally like!!

You must excuse this long scroll, as I have just finished my writing paper—it is what Father Christmas put in my stocking.

I hope all is well with you.

February 27th, 1917.

I am working hard for the exams. I saw by chance in the Orderly Room that one of my schemes was being sent to the Commandant, together with our underofficer's, as being super-excellent! A scheme is when we go out and draw maps of the country and then put our troops in various dispositions—to protect another force, for instance. We are doing night work to-night, and come back at nine o'clock. Then we get up at 6.30 again next day!

March 6th, 1917.

Great joy! A notice has come out to say that the College closes for three weeks from next Thursday, the day after to-morrow, and all cadets will return to their homes! We are going to be disinfected and sent home, "owing to the outbreak of mumps." This notice only came out this afternoon, and I am writing to tell you to expect me.

We are going to be disinfected in a steam and carbolic room. Very few mumps in our Company compared to the others.

The recess lasted for just under four weeks, and was a pure joy to all concerned. Christopher spent many days rabbit-shooting, starting out after a late breakfast with his lunch in his pocket in company with a keeper. He would return at dusk to a square meal, and afterwards every member of the family, big and little, would be summoned to an inspection of the bag, a row of brown bunnies of various sizes spread out upon stone flags. Each bunny would be commented on, often the place and manner of its shooting would be described in detail—the heaviest would be weighed—some would be tied together and labelled for despatching in various directions—the family and household having entered protests against a diet too exclusively rabbit.

Beethoven in the Music Room, followed by a pipe and much talk, usually completed the round of the day.

R.M.C., *April 8th*, 1917.

DEAREST MOTHER,—I got your letter last night—not to-day as you had expected. I have had a strange Easter—no church—but I have meditated upon things in heaven and earth generally.

We had a three hours' Law paper this morning, in which I did very well, I think, as I believe I got practically everything right. Then this afternoon we had a three-hours' paper on Administration, which I did not do so well, for this reason. Half the questions were on things we had not done with our officers, though we ought to have done them. However, I knew the other questions absolutely pat, so am sure of not having failed in it, and made very good common-sense tries for the ones we had not been taught. We have only three more exams. now, Physical Training, Musketry, and Drill. We had one oral paper, and I got 150, full marks, for that. The two officers who correct all our

company's papers and do our exams. are very nice—
one is Major Powell, and Captain Galsworthy—officers of another company. . . .

I might have still been here now without any recess
if it hadn't been for the mumps! I did enjoy my time
so much, and did more work, I think, than I should
have done had I been here. Harris has brought back a
stiletto which he can throw into a wall from a great
distance and it sticks there. I will write again soon;
we shall meet again in three weeks, and I hope I shall
get another recess then!

April 11*th*, 1917.

We have been having intervals of snow and hail all
to-day. Many thanks for the Wise One's cake. I will
write him a letter myself. I am sorry to have forgotten
that it was his birthday—but in the stress of exams.
I have had a lot to do.

We had a ten-mile route march yesterday (in the
middle of exams.!), but I was not very tired. I did a
lot of walking when I went shooting. I thought of
that book about the Foreign Legion where they did
thirty miles a day! We are now doing what is called
Company Training till we leave—that is work in the
open, and sort of sham fights every day. We practise
what we have learnt in theory, *i.e.*, attacking over
different sorts of ground, etc. We have to practise
lying down and getting up quickly; the gorse is very
prickly, and suddenly a whistle blows and we have to
fall down flat! There is probably going to be a Company Supper in London the day we pass out—that is,
all the seniors have a sort of final good-bye, and I have
said I will come.—Farewell.

Friday, April 20th, 1917.

DEAREST MOTHER,—All well here. We have been out every day this week so far, doing Field Days, and not coming back till after four. We have been having sham fights, etc., combined with route marches, but we have not been getting up early before breakfast, so it has not been so bad.

To-night we are going to practise relieving trenches, which is always carried out by night, and we leave the R.M.C. at 9.30 p.m., and stay in the trenches till 12 midnight. I hope to get back about 1 a.m.!!

Then next Wednesday the Duke of Connaught is coming down to inspect us. On the other days we are having Field Days of the whole Battalion together—about 1,000 strong.

Our G.S. tunics have all gone down to have Stars put on! . . .

God bless you, dear mother.—Ever your loving

CRUFF.

April 24th, 1917.

DEAREST MOTHER,—Just one line to say I have passed out twelfth—out of about 330 in the R.M.C. Tod very pleased, and gave me the list of everybody. Giles says I ought to order my uniform directly I leave; that is the usual thing to do.

I wrote to the Adjutant of the Welsh Guards yesterday on receipt of your telegram. I told him I should probably be reporting for duty about ten days after leaving here, as I think we may get ten days' recess, though it is not certain.

We have got our kit: it came yesterday, and I have

got a magnificent Welsh Guards sword, with leeks on it in every direction! Also I have got my tunic with stars on it, and a Sam Brown belt. . . .

Ever your loving

CRUFF.

He returned to Wales on April 30th, and was gazetted to the Welsh Guards on the same day. From the 7th to the 15th Mother and Son were in London, a time much occupied with visits to tailor, cap-maker, etc., but which gave opportunity for seeing a number of plays and hearing several operas. On May 15th he joined his Regiment at Tadworth, where it was in camp.

CHAPTER X

"Questa montágna è tale,
Che sempre al cominciar di sotto è grave,
E quanto uom più va su, e men fa male.
  Però quand' ella ti parrà soave
Tanto, che il su andar ti sia leggiero,
Come a seconda guiso andar per nave,
  Allor sarai al fin d'esto sentiero:
Quivi di riposar l'affano aspetta."

  "Tu sei sî presso all' ultima salute
. . . . che tu dei
Aver le luci tue chiare ed acute."
Dante, "Purgatorio," Canto iv.; "Paradiso," Canto xxii.

(See page 299.)

Guards' Camp, Tadworth, Surrey.
May 16*th*, 1917.

DEAREST MOTHER,—My address is as you see above
—though you had better put *Welsh* Guards in.

I will tell you all my adventures from the time I
left you. I got out at Tadworth and walked to the
camp, leaving my luggage at the station. Then I saw
the Adjutant—Martin Smith his name is—a nice man.
Then I went back to the station, got a cab, and brought
up my luggage. I was given a tent and a servant. He
unpacked my things. Then the furniture arrived from
Orpington,[1] and I got a bed (a proper one) and a chest

---

[1] Whence the Regiment had that day arrived at Tadworth.

of drawers and washing stand and looking glass and towel horse. I went to the ante-room, and we messed at 7.30. Webb[1] was away for the day, and I felt very lost at first, but by now I know all the Second-Lieutenants and some of the other officers. I think they are a very nice lot.

We had a good mess—with new potatoes!—and then I went to bed by the light of a lantern. We do not get up early except when we are on duty for the day. Breakfast at 8.15, parade at 9. I am in command of a platoon, with Llewellyn and Carlyon in command of the other platoons. Captain Taylor commands the Company. . . . We drilled from nine to ten. At ten we had Company Orderly Room, and soldiers were brought up before Taylor for various offences; we stood behind him. Some men were absent when they should not have been. Witnesses, etc., were called. One man "created a disturbance" after lights out—others had dirty buttons. Then we inspected the men's tents. From eleven to twelve we did more drill. Then we got off till two, lunch in between.

All the senior officers are very nice to me, and inquire affectionately about Sandhurst! . . . I find it a great advantage having been to Sandhurst. Webb came to see me early this morning. He is very nice to me, and we get on well together. I am an Ensign (i.e., Second-Lieutenant). A Subaltern is a full Lieutenant.

Then we get off at 3 p.m. and can go away if we

[1] At Kingsgate House, Winchester, with him. Since killed in action, December 1st, 1917.

like, as long as we get back at nine next morning, in time for parade. . . .

I have to inspect my platoon and look at their buttons. We did musketry from two to three to-day.

I want to impress upon you how happy I am here. It is much nicer than Sandhurst, and I feel certain I am going to enjoy it.

God bless you, mother dear, I did enjoy our time together!—Your loving   CRUFF.

Could you send me two pillow-cases (no sheets) and my woolly jacket, as it is cold here?   All well.

May 16th, 1917.

DEAREST MOTHER,—I am writing you a second letter just to tell you anything I think of.   I am in my tent, which is quite comfortable, thanks to my servant Charles, who is a Cardiff man.   I am so glad to have my Horace with me.   There is one Ode I know about soldiers in camp: I am looking for it, but have not been able to find it yet. . . .   The men in our Company are most of them fairly new, and only just past the recruit stage, so they are very slack just at present.   The officers' tents are in a field apart from the main body of the camp.   On parade for the first ten minutes all we do is that the officers commanding platoons march up and down, up and down, in front of the Company. The work is much slacker than Sandhurst.   Webb is doing a course of signalling, and knows the Morse code backwards now!

I thought of you arriving last night with your bunnies and felt so lonely and desperate at leaving you till I got here.   I know I shall be happy here and enjoy myself. My work is interesting, and it is a great advantage having been to Sandhurst and knowing my job. The floor of my tent is wood, and about 12 ft. in diameter. It was strange waking up and finding myself in a tent! The light penetrates the canvas quite early. I like the younger officers here very much, and I think I shall get on well with them. My Spotted Dog[1] is unpacked and empty, and I have got a nice large chest of drawers. I hope you are reading the "Ear of Dionysius"![2] I expect I shall hear from you to-morrow. . . . We only wear the khaki hats for parade, etc., here, and keep our super-magnificent hats for London. I am so glad I followed your advice and brought a box to keep my hat in! I often think you are wrong and find out afterwards that you are right— dear mother!—or rather, I now seldom disagree with you *re* anything!

We had a delicious time together. Give my love to everyone at Cadoxton. God bless you.—Ever your loving

CRUFF.

May 18*th*, 1917.

DEAREST MOTHER,—All well here. I am very happy and getting on splendidly. My work for the last two days has been to go round with the Picquet Officer (called Orderly Officer in line regiments), so as to learn a job which I shall shortly have to do my-

---

[1] An airtight uniform case, so-called from the peculiar decorations in paint on it.
[2] A paper on Automatic Writings, by Mr. G. W. Balfour, given to him during a recent visit to Fisher's Hill. (*Proceedings of the Society for Psychical Research,* part lxxiii., vol. xxix.)

self. It means turning out and inspecting the guard of the camp at 12.30 p.m. and 11 p.m. in the evening, also attending parades of men doing punishments at two and four o'clock. Then visiting the cook-house and men's dinners, asking if there are any complaints, and a number of other minor things. It also involves getting up at 6 a.m. to be at the 6.40 breakfast parade. I have to do this three days running. The Picquet Officer is not allowed to leave the camp while on duty. There is not much other news to tell you, except that I have been drilled a bit in a squad of private soldiers—but I did all that at Sandhurst, so I know it all right. Every officer on joining starts by having to do this. We have a very good mess here—everything very hot, and cream at lunch!—also lump sugar and potatoes!

All the officers are very nice to me, and I get on well with the Second-Lieutenants, who are my equals. The Scots, Coldstream and Grenadier Guards are all coming here, and some of the officers of each regiment will mess in the same tent with us. Ever your loving
CRUFF.

May 21*st*, 1917.

DEAREST MOTHER,—I have got my clubs and racket safely. Many thanks for sending them. I have not been doing much of interest lately, beyond what I told you in my last letter. On Sunday we had church parade, which I attended, as I was on, duty that day. We had a sort of service in the open air, sitting on benches. The men sang most beautifully—in harmony. There was a funny little padre who seemed very optimistic about everything, and was full of "All's right with the world" ideas. After that I and another officer were taken to a place about five miles off by one of the officers, who invited me over. We went over by car to this house of his, which belongs to him. There was nobody there except a cook and a housekeeper, and we had a nice lunch and then played billiards and gramophones, and walked about in his garden. We left at 4.30, as we had to be back by dinner.

Please send me all the manuscript notebooks written in my own handwriting, which went back to Wales in my trunk. They are *essential* to me. We have got two Volunteer Officers who have just joined to do some training. One is a Captain and one a Lieutenant, but I am senior to them! Tremendous thunderstorms, and torrents of rain coming into the tents last night, but to-day fine. All well here. I am well and happy. —Ever your loving

CRUFF.

May 23rd, 1917.

All well here. I went up to London yesterday with Webb, and we went to a theatre and came down that evening.

There are about fifteen other Welsh Guards officers here. The Grenadiers have just come, in number about twenty officers. The Welsh Guards officers consist of: Colonel Stracey Clitherow; Captains: Marshall Roberts, Aldridge (a Wykehamist), and Taylor; Lieutenants: Martin Smith (Adjutant), Howard,[1] Dickens,

[1] Lieut. the Hon. Philip Fitzalan Howard, died of wounds, May 21st, 1918.

de Wiart; Second Lieutenants: Webb,[1] Pryce, Llewellyn, Mathew, Gore, Byrne [2] and Baness (just left for the front), Carlyon and myself. In my platoon there are a large number of Davies, Evans, Jones, Griffiths, Bowens, etc., so most of them are Welsh. I have not come across any Neath men. We do not always sit in the same places at mess, but move about. I generally go and sit next to one of my friends. I feel well and am very fit.. I am going to get some riding, as we borrow horses from the senior officers. After mess we usually sit and read or talk; mess is over about 9.15. I have played bridge, too, and bézique. Letters are put in pigeon-holes in the ante-room by Sergeant James (formerly policeman at Port Talbot). I have not been able to get a *Daily News*. Do you think I could get it posted from London? I called on Stracey Clitherow to-day and had tea with him. . . . Tadworth has no village that I can find. There is a station, and a few houses round, with, I believe, one or two small shops. I keep my bike in a shed, locked up.

I am now drilling the men every day. Yesterday I took a parade of about 200 men!

The Brigadier-General in command of this Brigade has asked for a map of some trenches which have been dug near here, and I have been chosen by the Commanding Officer of the Welsh Guards to make this map. I have got all day to-morrow for it; we did that sort of thing at Sandhurst. All well here. I fear I shall be unable to go up to London for this week-end, as I am almost certain to be on duty.

[1] Mr. Webb was killed in action, December 1st, 1917.
[2] Mr. Byrne was killed in action, March 9th, 1918.

May 25th, 1917.

This morning I passed off in Squad Drill under the Adjutant's eye! I had to drill a squad of men, giving the commands on the proper foot, etc., and I managed this all right. Then this afternoon I had to pay the Company! Any mistake I made would have to be made up out of my own pocket, but to-day I got the sum exactly right. Many thanks for my books, which have arrived safely. I shall be doing Company Drill now.

I have been up to London the last few days, going up in the afternoon and coming back in the evening. I got the Regimental Adjutant, Crawshay (Williams Bulkeley is away), to take me to the Guards' Club, where I have been introduced. My *Daily News* comes every morning, and is a great joy to me. It is nice our reading the same things. I see a letter from you in to-day's *Times re* Pensions. I played tennis yesterday with the Adjutant here, Martin Smith, and got on very well; we played at a house near here. He is one of the Smiths, of the Union of London and Smiths Bank, and knows the Serocolds and all about them. I will write again at greater length, am on parade now.

June 6th, 1917.

I am getting on well here, and am very happy. The map of the trenches I made was a great success, and General Monck sent for me and congratulated me on it. He made me write my name on it, and is going to have it copied and given to each unit.

To-morrow Lord French is coming down to inspect us, and we have been rehearsing to-day for it. He will inspect the whole Brigade in a large field near the camp. I am Picquet Officer to-day, and have just come off a large parade, where I inspected defaulters. I took memoranda to-day and dealt out punishments to the men, tempering justice with mercy!

*Guards' Club, S.W.*1, *June* 13*th*, 1917.

DEAREST MOTHER,—I have not written for some time because I have been most frightfully busy. I was up here the week-end, and went back to Tadworth Sunday evening. The next morning at six my servant woke me, saying I was to be at Chelsea Barracks at 9 a.m., so I caught a train up to London, travelling with another man, Llewellyn, who is doing a bombing course.

I am doing the Lewis machine-gun course. The gun is automatic, and fires 400 shots per minute, and is used a great deal by the infantry. Every officer does this course. It will be over on Friday, and I am going down to Fisher's Hill on Saturday for the week-end.

We work from nine to twelve, and two to five; then we have to copy out notes in the evening, so there is a great deal to do. We are taught by a Sergeant, about ten Officers, three others in the Brigade of Guards, but none in my Regiment.

The cuttings you sent me I saw in the papers—all except the one about the officers complaining *re* manners of Guardsmen. The reason of that is that the attitude of some of the Brigade to officers of the line is like that of a large and magnificent lion to an obscure blackbeetle!

I will write at greater length to-morrow.—Your loving   CRUFF.

Fisher's Hill, Woking, June 17th, 1917.

I am enjoying myself here very much. On Friday I did my exam. on the Lewis gun; the exam. was in two parts, part written and part oral. The marks we got for the oral were read out before we left. (I got full marks for oral, and one other officer only!) We shall hear the whole result next Saturday. On Wednesday I dined with Llewellyn, and we went to the play together.

Delicious weather here—warm and sunny—garden looking lovely and full of scents. . . .

You said you were enclosing a list of books for me to get from Mudie's, but it was not enclosed in your letter. Shall I get "Varieties of Religious Experience," by William James?—God bless you.

Guards' Camp, Tadworth, Surrey.
June 18th.

I got back here safely last night. Many thanks for Wells's book.[1] I shall start reading it to-day. This morning I have been sitting on a court-martial, but may not divulge anything about it to anyone yet!

I shall think of you walking in the Eisteddfod Procession! I do hope the Commanding Officer will give me leave for the Gorsedd.

God bless you, dear mother. You are often in my thoughts. I have been very busy the last week, but now shall be able to write more frequently. The father of two Wykehamists in my house is now here as a volunteer officer—we have to instruct him. Rather killing, this!

[1] "God the Invisible King."

June 22nd, 1917.

DEAREST MOTHER,—I have got leave for the Gorsedd! and shall arrive Wednesday evening at 7.55, I hope, and return by the train leaving Neath at 3.55 on Friday. This is the longest I can get—but it will be very nice. Fox-Pitt, the Adjutant, persuaded the Commanding Officer to let me go! All well here. My work is now entirely field work, attacking and defending positions in the country, with my platoon. There is a draft going out to France next week. It is nice here now, and not too hot.

I am rejoicing over Women's Suffrage. It is splendid that it has come at last.

I am getting the blue evening uniform and the grey great-coat. The blue is worn on ceremonial occasions, and chiefly when dining in London. It is the evening "dress" of khaki. I went up to London with Webb yesterday. In the evening Webb took me to a revue called "Bubbly," which was very amusing. I hope all is well with you at Cadoxton.

The following note on the Gorsedd Circle, by the Revd. Mardy Rees, is here reprinted (slightly abbreviated) with the author's permission:

The Gorsedd (throne) circle is exciting a good deal of interest; and English friends frequently ask what is the origin and meaning of the Gorsedd. It has been said that the circle represents a temple of religion, a court of justice, the twelve counties of Wales, and so forth. Personally, we believe that its chief purpose was astronomical. It takes us back four thousand years at least, to the days when there were no clocks or almanacks. The Druids were able by means of the stones in the circle to tell the time of night as well as of the day, and

CHRISTOPHER—JULY, 1917.
WELSH GUARDS SECTION.

of the year. They watched the clock stars, especially the Pleiades, which became visible about an hour before sunrise on May 1st. This was important, as they offered a sacrifice at sunrise at that season of the year. The stones also gave people the points of the compass.

The Druids kept the secrets themselves, and only the initiated knew them. They died, but the secrets have been discovered by later generations. A great authority on the Gorsedd states that the principles of the ancient circle are incorporated in every old parish church in the country. The church took the place of the Gorsedd.

Sir Norman Lockyer believes that the Welsh circle contained all the characteristic features of several Egyptian temples. He refers to the Temple of Amen-Ra, with its avenue of stone pillars, a quarter of a mile long. At the end of the avenue, in a darkened chamber, was the image of Ra. Once in the year, about June 21st, at set of sun, a golden shaft of light would strike the face of the image in this chamber, and the worshippers believed that they had seen the face of their god. It was a natural phenomenon, but only the priests knew that. This chamber was situated where the two outside pillars of stone stand to-day, in the Gorsedd circle.

There is an old Welsh tradition that he who spends a night in the mystic circle will be either a bard or a lunatic. In other words, a son of the light or darkness. The throne of the bard is very old. It is anterior to that of the king or bishop. Civilisation has dethroned the bard, but he still holds his place in the life of the Nation.

The Proclamation of the National Eisteddfod of the year 1918 by the Gorsedd of the Bards was held in Neath on June 28th. It was a memorable day for that ancient town. Those who were to take part in the Procession to the Gorsedd Circle assembled in the robing room, where a large number of Bards wearing their robes awaited them. Here the regalia, consisting of the Gorsedd sword, banner, divided sword, and Hirlas horn, was set out in readiness to be borne through the streets. The Hirlas horn, presented by Lord Tredegar in 1897, was designed by Herkomer, and is one of the most beautiful of Welsh treasures. Headed by a band, the Procession wended its way through the principal streets of the town—which now, alas! like so many centres of industrial life, shows little trace of its past history.

In Roman times Nidium was an important place on the Via Julia, and in the Middle Ages it played a no mean part in Welsh history. The castle is said to have been built in 1090 by Richard de Granville, one of the twelve Norman Knights of Robert Fitzhamon, the conqueror of Glamorgan. In 1231 the castle was captured by Llewellyn, Prince of North Wales, who is said to have razed it to the ground and to have exterminated the inhabitants. It was afterwards rebuilt, and Edward II., while passing through South Wales raising forces to contend against his rebellious Queen, Isabella, was captured and imprisoned within its walls. To-day only the portcullis gate and towers remain standing.

Neath is one of the most ancient boroughs in the country, a charter having been granted to the burgesses by one of the Earls of Gloucester as far back as the twelfth century. The ruins of Neath Abbey—once "the fairest abbey in all Wales"—lie a mile to the west of the town. Founded in 1129 for Grey Friars, it was granted at its dissolution in 1539 to Sir Richard Williams, alias Cromwell, a great-grandfather of the Protector.

After perambulating the main streets, crowded with miners from the neighbouring valleys, the Gorsedd Procession (in which Christopher took part, walking immediately before the Gorsedd Banner) made its way to the Bardic Circle, fourteen great monoliths set up to form a large circle round a fine central logan. These stones had for the most part been presented by the landowners of the district. Christopher had taken a special interest in searching for and deciding on a stone to be given from the Tennant Estate. The stones must be untouched by chisel, of a certain height and size, and it was long before one was found which satisfied the requirements of the Gorsedd and the individual taste of members of the family.

One was discovered at last, over 6 feet high and about 18 inches broad, lying partly covered with earth in the woods on the hillside above Cadoxton Lodge, a great grey block of Pennant rock, the local stone of the county.

It had been set up, together with the other thirteen stones, in the Victoria Gardens, and there the proclamation that the National Eisteddfod of Wales of 1918 would be held in Neath took place.

The old decree runs: "The Gorsedd and Chair of the Bards of the Isle of Britain shall be held in the face of the Sun and Eye of Light, and in the free open sky, so that it may be seen and heard of all."

After the sounding of the Corn Gwlad, or Trumpet of the Fatherland, the Gorsedd Prayer was offered by one of the Bards. It may be translated as follows:

"Give us, O God, Thy protection,
And in Thy protection strength,
And in strength understanding,
And in understanding to know,
And in knowing the knowledge of the Righteous One,
And in knowing Him to love Him,
And in loving Him to love every essential being,
And in loving every essential being to love God and every
    goodness."

Standing on the central Logan Stone in his robes, the Archdruid made the Proclamation, and was presented with the Cup of Welcome. Addresses by the Bards, interspersed with Penillion singing to the accompaniment of the harp, followed. It was a moving scene. Within the circle stood the Bards in their bright-coloured robes. Ringed around it was a seated crowd, including a large number of girls wearing the Welsh national costume; beyond, again, a vast mass of men and women stood, and the amphitheatre of hills rose upwards half veiled in the haze of a perfect summer's day.

Few of those present will ever forget the moment when, the whole audience rising to its feet and every man in uniform standing rigid at attention, the National Anthem of Wales, *Hen Wlad fy Nhadau*, burst forth in volumes of glorious sound, rising and falling on the air—sung as only a Welsh crowd sings, in harmony and with pure and perfect intonation. It was the climax of a day charged with deep emotion.

Cymru am byth!

It was Christopher's passionate desire that the Welsh Guards should become officially connected with the annual celebration of the National Eisteddfod, and his fixed determination was to work towards the establishment of such a tradition at the ensuing Eisteddfod, which was to be held in his native town. Though he did not live to do the work he had contemplated, it was carried on by other hands, and as a result the Regiment was for the first time officially represented at the National Eisteddfod of 1918. Colonel Murray-Threipland, D.S.O., commanding the Welsh Guards, the Regimental Adjutant, Captain the Earl of Lisburne, Captain Fox-Pitt, M.C., and Lieut. G. C. H. Crawshay, were present as official guests, and, together with close upon a hundred men of the Regiment, took part in the Gorsedd and other ceremonies held in connection with the National Festival. The Regimental Male Voice Choir competed in the Male Voice Choral Competition, being placed second in order of merit by the Adjudicators, and receiving a great ovation from the vast crowd of over ten thousand people assembled in the Pavilion. Within the Gorsedd Circle one of the most eloquent of the addresses delivered from the Maen Llôg (the great central Logan Stone) called upon Welshmen to remember Christopher Tennant, who had stood within that Circle when the Eisteddfod was proclaimed, as the type of patriot which young Welshmen should desire to emulate.

Writing of the events of those days, one of his brother-officers who took part in them sums up his impressions in the following words:—

"August 13*th,* 1918.

"To me, at least, the whole Eisteddfod programme seemed to centre round Christopher. I couldn't help feeling that in spirit he was present, and that he knew his ambition to see the Regiment represented at Neath had been realised. I know that the wonderful reception we received on mounting the platform was intended just as much for him, and the others who are with him, as it was intended for those who were actually the subject of it. You remember that when I first wrote to you I said that his great sacrifice would not be in vain; and already his influence is being felt. Let us hope that generations of Welshmen will follow him in the example he set, by pride of race and nobility of character."

Saturday, June 30th.

DEAREST MOTHER,—I got back safely yesterday, and everyone was much interested in the Gorsedd. I gave Fox-Pitt a glowing account!

I am going on a bombing course, starting Monday, and it lasts a fortnight. I shall be sleeping at Richmond Terrace every night. The course is at ten, and is over at three every day. No time for more.—Ever your loving

CRUFF.

On July 5th his mother joined him in London. Their first excitement was the daylight air-raid on July 7th, in which both found themselves in positions of considerable "liveliness," though in widely separated localities. *Tannhäuser* in the afternoon and Brieux's *Three Daughters of M. Dupont* in the evening closed a rather strenuous day. On the 9th the photograph of Christopher included in this volume was taken by Beresford.

The Recruiting Exemptions Committee was at this time sitting in the Grand Committee Room of the House of Commons, and a long afternoon was spent there, his Mother's work on the Neath Rural District War Pensions Committee having roused the keen interest of the family in the questions upon which the Committee was then taking evidence.

The ritual of ices at Gunter's was not forgotten (p.

92). Two characteristic incidents belong to this period. Walking one day with his mother through Westminster Cathedral and examining the beautiful mosaics and marbles of the side chapels, Christopher noted that whereas chapels of St. George, St. Andrew and St. Patrick were to be found, none appeared to have been dedicated to St. David. Striding up to the lady chapel, he sought a priest, and, saying he was "from Wales," inquired where the chapel of his patron saint was situated. On being informed that none at present existed, he expressed his surprise and regret in very plain language, leaving the priest in visible bewilderment as to who this young giant from Wales could be.

Is it too much to hope that as a memorial to the sons of Wales fallen in the war a replica of Goscombe John's beautiful statue of St. David, presented to the City Hall, Cardiff, by Lord Rhondda, may be set up in one of the side chapels of Westminster Cathedral?

Equally characteristic was an incident in connection with the purchase of an automatic pistol at the Army and Navy Stores. It was necessary to obtain a permit before one could be supplied, and this involved the filling up of an official form. Instructed by the foreman of the Gun Department, Christopher was successfully negotiating its intricacies until they came to the space reserved for "Nationality." "Put 'English' there, sir," said the foreman. "English! but I'm not English," the boy answered, flushing; and in the space reserved he inked in in capital letters, the word "WELSH."

One week-end and another long Sunday were spent with the beloved "Aunt Betty" of the letters, Lady Betty Balfour, at Fisher's Hill, near Woking, where the garden was at its loveliest and the Surrey commons which surround it gay with field flowers.

Both in the Lewis gun course and in the bombing course Christopher obtained a first.

Tadworth, July 16th, 1917.

I arrived here safely last night, feeling very lonesome at having to part from you. I travelled down with Fox-Pitt. There are two new Ensigns, but I have not seen much of them yet; they come from Wales, I think. I shall be on Sunday duty next Sunday, I fear, which means dining in Saturday and Sunday evening. However, I am trying hard to get someone to do it for me, and I will let you know if I succeed. It is quite possible I shall get someone. I went out this morning with the Training Company, who dug trenches. This afternoon I took 2 o'clock parade of the Company. Carlyon is going to the front next week, and has just gone on a few days' leave. Everything is much the same as when I left. We are having night operations to-morrow. Major Dene is back and in command of the Company. I enjoyed our time so much, especially Fisher's Hill at the end. Even if I cannot get off Sunday duty, I shall try and come for the afternoon, as I must see you once more before you go to Wales. . . .

July 7th, 1917.

DEAREST MOTHER,—I have wired you to-day, as I can come next week-end, having got someone else to do Sunday duty for me. My blue hat has turned up from the Lost Property Office at Waterloo! I must have left it in the train, and am glad to get it back.

I have been writing in my Red Book (which you gave me) partly autobiography and partly meditations on various subjects—which you must read some day.[1]

We were to have had Regimental Sports to-day with our own Welsh Guards band, but they have put it off, as it is raining.

All well here. We had a lecture on Tactics this morning by Marshall Roberts.—Ever your loving

CRUFF.

July 19th, 1917.

We had Regimental Sports to-day—I enclose programme. I ran in the Officers' Race (100 yards). It is item 20 on the list, and gave much pleasure to the men! One got a yard's start for each year's service. Marshall Roberts had sixteen yards' start—and won the race! I was sixth. The band came down from London and played; it was delicious.

July 28th, 1917.

I went to a dance yesterday evening, which I enjoyed immensely. It was given by our Regimental Adjutant, Crawshay. He is now a great friend of mine.

All sorts of interesting people were there, and I danced the whole time with various people. All well here. I am going to Winchester to-morrow.

[1] *See* pp. 104 and 113.

July 31*st*, 1917.

I enjoyed my visit to Winchester very much—everybody there very cordial and pleased to see me—especially Monte. I had brew[1] with the prefects. Webb did not come, as he has gone on draft leave. It has been pouring with rain here all day and all last night, but I am well and happy.

The Commanding Officer has told me to be inoculated this week, here, by the doctor attached to our Regiment. He has got all the stuff, etc. There is no news to tell you. I read the *Daily News* every day, which I get regularly. How amusing the people at Neath mistaking me for the Prince of Wales! I enjoyed the dance very much. I am quite a good dancer, and enjoy it. People only dance one-steps and fox-trots nowadays, with a waltz occasionally. I can dance all those.

On August 2nd he arrived home on draft leave. Those who have passed through such days know all there is to be known of their poignant sweetness and agony; those to whom such days have not come can only dimly understand.

Home is enfolding its children together, perhaps for the last time; youth must fare forth to unnumbered and unknown dangers, while love can only stay behind, to stand and wait. Elderly folk who have watched the baby pass into childhood, from childhood to boyhood, and from boyhood to the first stage of early manhood, come to take leave of their lad—their

[1] Tea.

sense of possession in him strong with the links which country life, perhaps, alone can give; small brothers are round-eyed and troubled at the general stir and at the news that he who is half their world is "going to the war."

Pilgrimages are made to places round which happy memories are twined. Silences fall, too precious to be broken "by fragmentary speech."

> "Since in that hour the still souls held as nought
> The body's beauty or brain's responsive thought,
> Content to feel that life in life had grown
> Separate no longer, but one life alone;
> Ay, and they guessed thereby what life shall be
> When Love world-wide has shown his mystery."

And mixed with all this sense of the mystery and the beauty and the tragedy of life is the necessity of clear-headed Martha-ing over details of kit and equipment. It was during these days that Mother and Son arranged together what each would do and each would aim at if the seeming separation of bodily death rose suddenly between them.[1] The days were very full, but time was snatched for walks to places beloved on hillside and in wood; the evenings brought the comfort of Bee-thoven sonatas; and some special treasures of English literature were shared again by reading aloud:—E. B. B.'s "Sonnets from the Portuguese," vi., which was the keynote of the parting; Kettle's lovely lines to his little daughter written "In the Field before Guillemont,

---

[1] *See* Chap. IV.

Somme, September 4th, 1916," ending with those ringing words on the fallen—who

"Died not for flag, nor king, nor emperor,
But for a dream, born in a herdsman's shed,
And for the Secret Scripture of the Poor."

Also a splendid poem by Ralph Hodgson, "The Song
of Honour," new to Christopher, which made a great
impression upon him; and, at his special wish, the letter written by Mr. Britling after his own son's death
to the old German couple who were the parents of
Herr Heinrich, in the last chapter of Wells's master-
piece. "Our sons who have shown us God. . . ."

On Bank Holiday, August 6th, Christopher left his
home for the last time. Of all the farewells of those
last days this was the only one which moved him to
outward expression of emotion. The old Welsh house
in that far-away Welsh valley held for him something
of the essence, as it were, of his own being; and to leave
it was a "death in life" which cut him to the quick.
Pater's words best describe the link which bound him
to it:

"The house in which she lives is for the orderly soul which
does not live on blindly before her, but is ever, out of her
passing experiences, building and adorning the parts of a
many-roomed abode for herself, only an expansion of the
body; as the body is but an expansion of the soul. For such
an orderly soul, as she lives onward, all sorts of delicate affini-
ties establish themselves, between her and the doors and pas-
sage-ways, the lights and shadows of her outward abode, until
she seems incorporate into it—till at last, in the entire expres-
siveness of what is outward, there is for her, to speak properly,

no longer any distinction between outward and inward at all; and the light which creeps at a particular hour on a wall, the scent of flowers in the air at a particular window, become to her, not so much apprehended objects, as themselves powers of apprehension, and doorways to things beyond—seeds or rudiments of new faculties, by which she, dimly yet surely, apprehends a matter lying beyond her actually attained capacity of sense and spirit."

His mother travelled with him to London, and there two strenuous days were spent in collecting the necessary items of Active Service kit and equipment. On the Wednesday morning he returned to Tadworth and heard that he was to cross to France on the morrow with a draft of about 150 men of the Welsh Guards, the other officer in charge being Lieut. R. W. Hargreaves. Obtaining a few hours' leave, he returned to London and rejoined his mother, travelling back to Tadworth again in the evening.

On Thursday, August 9th, they met at Waterloo Station and had forty minutes together. The draft had come up from Tadworth by train, and the men were lined up and marched to the platform from which they were to entrain for Southampton. A finer body of Welshmen it would have been hard to find. The air rang with the sound of their voices, the beautiful melodies of Aberystwith, "The Men of Harlech," "Hen Wlad fy Nhadau," making "a sunshine in the shady place." Ordinary travellers who found themselves in the station had the delight of listening to a male-voice choir giving an impromptu concert.

Six officers of the Welsh Guards left for the front

on that day. Lieut. R. W. Hargreaves and Sec.-Lieut. G. C. S. Tennant in charge of the draft, and Sec.-Lieuts. Webb, Devereux, Ballard, and Llewellyn travelling separately. Of these six, four have been killed in action: G. C. S. Tennant on September 3rd, R. W. Hargreaves and T. H. B. Webb on December 1st, and C. P. Ballard on March 10th, 1918. Sec.-Lieut. Devereux has been wounded and sent home, and Sec.-Lieut. Paul Llewellyn was dangerously wounded in March, 1918; so that of the six not one remains, at the time of writing, on active service.

CHAPTER XI

ON ACTIVE SERVICE

"Burningly it came on me all at once,
　　This was the place! . . .

What in the midst lay but the Tower itself? . . .

. . . noise was everywhere! it tolled
　　Increasing like a bell.　Names in my ears
　　Of all the lost adventurers my peers,—
How such a one was strong, and such was bold,
And such was fortunate, yet each of old
　　Lost, lost! one moment knelled the woe of years.

There they stood, ranged along the hillsides, met
　　To view the last of me, a living frame
　　For one more picture! in a sheet of flame
I saw them and I knew them all.　And yet
Dauntless the slug-horn to my lips I set,
　　And blew.　'*Childe Roland to the Dark Tower came.*' "
　　　　ROBERT BROWNING, "Childe Roland."

Guards' Division, Base Depot, B.E.F., France.
　　　　　　August 10th, 1917.

DEAREST MOTHER,—I have just arrived at the Base, and have been unable to wire so far, but may do so later if I can.

We censor our own letters here!

When I left you we went straight to Southampton. After waiting about an hour we embarked there—no weighing of kits, etc.

I was very distressed at having to leave you, but I expect we shall be here for some time. We left Southampton about four o'clock yesterday, but did not really do the crossing till night.

I slept on deck in my sleeping bag and on the airbed. Hobbs is a very efficient servant.

We missed the tide coming here, so we could not land in France till about 3 p.m. to-day, Friday. There were a lot of American officers on board. The boat was quite a large one, the ———. It had been a German one, and was captured from them. We had quite a smooth crossing, and nobody was ill.

Then we disembarked and marched to the Camp, about five or six miles off from where we disembarked. The roads were rough, and people sold us apples and chocolate on the way. Then we got here. It is a very large Camp, and there are officers whom I know in other Regiments of the Brigade.

The men are cheerful and happy. I expect to be here for some time. . . . We have a lot of Orders, etc., to read, and I will write again when I know more. I share a tent with Hargreaves.[1] Other officers are in huts. I will write again soon. God bless you.— Your loving   CRUFF.

> *August* 10*th*, 1917.
> *Second letter.*

I have got a tent with Hargreaves, and Hobbs has put out all my bed, etc. It is very like being in camp at Tadworth, here. We are allowed into the town (there are trams), but must not be there after 10 p.m.

---

[1] Killed in action, December 1st, 1917.

Llewellyn, Webb, and Ballard are here, but Hargreaves and I do all the work with the draft, and they are separate.

I really expect to be here about a month. I hear the Kaiser says the war will be over in three weeks!

You are all constantly in my thoughts. You must imagine me in Camp here—just like Tadworth, and perfectly safe—for some time—though the work is harder.

There are large notices everywhere cautioning us against spies. I shall soon find out the ropes, though everything is rather strange at first. We are high up here, and can see the sea in the distance. Good-night, mother dear. All well here. Do you remember Goff, who was at West Downs? He is here in the Scots Guards. I shall write again when I have more details to tell you. The Picquet Officer censors all the letters. A long job that, I should imagine. Write and tell me all you want to know. I can write with a great sense of privacy, being my own censor! God bless you.

Guards' Division, Base Depot, B.E.F.
August 12th, 1917.

We are allowed to say that we are at camp in Harfleur, near Havre. We have got 150 men. Hargreaves and I belong to this draft, but the other officers are separate.

I went into Havre yesterday with Llewellyn, and we sat in cafés and talked French at great length— at least I did—Llewellyn can't speak French. Then we had tea at a café, and I also had my hair cut—

the barber put all sorts of unguents on! I enjoy talking French to the inhabitants of Havre!

August 14*th*, 1917.

DEAREST MOTHER,—All well here. Yesterday we had a long day of training at the Camp. We did gas all day, and we all went through poison gas with respirators on.

On Sunday we had Church in the morning, and I attended the parade. Hargreaves has been warned that he will go up to the Entrenching Battalion, just behind the front lines, shortly, and I now go out in command of our draft (150)! The men are a splendid lot, and I have been able to get to know them better over here—privates and N.C.O.'s.

On Sunday I went into Havre and talked French at great length. That sort of practice makes me much more familiar with the language.

August 15*th*, 1917.

DEAREST MOTHER,—I am leaving here this evening and going straight to the 1st Battalion. All our officers (except Llewellyn who is in hospital—I don't know what is the matter with him) are going straight up to the 1st Battalion, and not to the Entrenching Battalion at all. Hobbs is coming with me. He was here last year, and says it took him three days to get up to the front. The train used to go so slowly that people got out and walked along, and then caught it up and got in again! It may be quicker getting up now. I am not sure where our 1st Battalion is. Probably resting, I should think. I expect our letters will be censored up there. We start at 6.30 p.m. to-day, and I will write again as soon as we reach our destination.

My eye is quite all right this morning; the swelling has gone down completely on the eyelid, and I have not been bitten by any more mosquitoes.

Well, dear Mother, you are ever in my thoughts, and you know what I feel, better than I can express it. I know you will be with me all through the coming days, and our love can bridge all distances.

Do not be anxious or worried; I know I shall return safe to you. I shall write to you constantly, and think of you all at Cadoxton. Give my love to Deedooge. God bless you, Mother dear. I shall take great care of myself, and come through everything all right.— Ever your loving and affectionate

CHRISTOPHER.

August 17*th*, 1917.

I am writing from a place *en route*.[1] We left the base on Wednesday evening, and travelled all night. I slept in the train. In the morning we reached a town the name of which I must not say.[2] It is a delicious quaint place. I went over the Cathedral—*most* lovely. We had a few hours there, and who do you think I met in the street but Betty Haggard?[3] She was very pleased to see me, but I had not time to see much of her.

[1] Etaples.   [2] Rouen.
[3] The widow of Captain Mark Haggard, Welsh Regiment, killed in action September, 1914. His dying cry, "Stick it, the Welsh!" will never be forgotten in the Principality. Christopher had spent many happy days with Mrs. Haggard before her marriage, at the home of her parents in the Vale of Neath.

Then we travelled the rest of the day and all the night, during which we slept. I went on the engine for part of the way and talked to the engine-driver.

We got here this morning, and are leaving soon. I do not know our destination. Must stop now.

August 18*th*, 1917.

All well here. We have arrived at our destination.[1] I wrote to you *en route* on Friday. Well, we travelled on to railhead, and from there were taken to the Reinforcement Camp in motor lorries, jolted all the way! We spent that night in the Camp, which has a small farmhouse for the officers to feed in. I conversed in French with the inhabitants, and then slept in a tent. This morning we had to walk up here, getting a lift in a lorry part of the way. We are now *out* of the line, and the Battalion was up a little time ago. I will write to you at greater length *re* all the new people I meet of the 1st Battalion. We are now at our destination for the moment. I have lost my fountain pen. Could you send me out another?—medium nib. Your two letters I got here this morning saying you had not yet heard. Must stop. Will write again.

August 18*th*. *Second letter.*

DEAREST MOTHER,—I wrote to you a few hours ago, a hurried letter. There are four Companies in the Battalion. I am in the first one, called The Prince of Wales's Company—it is the best in the Battalion,

[1] Petworth Camp, Proven.

and the Battalion is the best in the Army, so I could not wish for better.[1]

There are several officers here whom I knew at Tadworth.

To His Father.

August 19th, 1917.

DEAREST DEEDOOGE,—I have not written to you very lately, but you have been much in my thoughts. . . .

You will have heard most of my news from my letters to Mummy. As a matter of fact I am now in Flanders—I may tell you that much—and a little way behind the line. Last night we suddenly had the order all lights out about 10 p.m., and we were told the German aeroplanes were over; we heard bombs dropping about a mile off, and saw shrapnel bursting. It looked like little stars which came and then disappeared. The Germans come over round here fairly often, they say. We can hear the guns firing at night from here, though only faintly.

This morning I was sitting in my tent after breakfast when I heard a commotion, and rushed out just in time to see one of our aeroplanes, which was at a good height, turn nose downwards and fall with a crash. It was a wonderful sight. The aeroplane fell very rapidly, and landed about half a mile away. I do not know what the cause of it was. I may not tell you where we shall be when we go up into the line; I do not know really where we shall go to. Last time we were up north of blank and south of blank! and

[1] The Motto of the Company is, "Y ddraig goch a ddyry gychwyn." (The Red Dragon will give the lead.)

north-west of somewhere else—where the Germans were very pressing.[1] Martin Smith is out here, but he is not Adjutant.

One of our Sergeants has been recommended for the V.C., but I do not know if he has got it yet.

In case you should know any of them, our officers are:

Commanding Officer	COL. DOUGLAS GORDON.
Second in Command	MAJOR LUXMORE BALL.
Captains	GIBBS.
	LORD LISBURNE.
	RODERICK.[2]
	BATTYE.
	TAYLOR.
Subalterns	MARTIN SMITH.
	NEWALL.[3]
	MENZIES.
	HARGREAVES.[4]
Ensigns	DEVAS (Adjutant).
	SHAND.
	FRIPP.
	LASCELLES.
	BYRNE.[5]

And those who came out with me. Also de Satgé, Interpreter (was a master at Eton).

I am in the Prince of Wales's Company. It is always known by that name, and never as No. 1 Company.

[1] Words used by Raymond Lodge to signify Ypres. *See* "Raymond," p. 17.
[2] Killed in action, December 1st, 1917.
[3] Killed in action, October 12th, 1917.
[4] Killed in action, December 1st, 1917.
[5] Killed in action, March 9th, 1918.

I hope all is well with you; I long to hear from you, dearest Deedooge. I got a book at the station to read—"Woodstock," by Scott. Do you know it? Farewell.—Your loving

CHRISTOPHER.

P.S.—I played cricket for the Prince of Wales's Company yesterday, and am playing again this afternoon.

Sunday, August 19th, 1917, 10 a.m.

DEAREST MOTHER,—The General of the Division (Feilding is his name) is coming down this morning to present decorations, etc., to various men, but now he cannot come, so we are only having a church parade this morning. The padre here is a good fellow (Mogg) and has a sense of humour—an excellent thing in padres!

I did so enjoy your two letters—I know all you feel, and you know what I feel. I long to be with you, but here I am happy, and I like the other officers, and I shall have lots to tell you that I cannot tell you now. We get ten days about every three months, so I shall be back soon, and we can get leave to Paris occasionally. You could come over to Paris! . . .

Many thanks for that lovely poem [1]—which I shall keep. I get my <i>Daily News</i>, which is a great joy, as there are no papers provided here. We mess in a small farm, and I sleep in a tent which I am sharing with one Bonsor, who is in Paris at present. The men are very wonderful—everyone says so—and very <i>Welsh.</i>

[1] Ebenezer Elliot's hymn, "When wilt Thou save the people?" <i>See</i> p. 172.

August 20*th*, 1917.

DEAREST MOTHER,—All well. . . . Llewellyn is still at the Base in hospital with some sort of fever. He is not seriously ill at all.

Now for my news. Yesterday I played cricket in the afternoon for the Prince of Wales's Company. In the evening German aeroplanes again came over, and one we saw some way off detected by searchlights, which all focussed on him, and shrapnel bursting all round—a wonderful sight. He got away, however!

This morning my Company Commander returned, and I like him very much. His name is Gibbs, and he is very human and affectionate (not the typical soldier type), and I am told he has simply *made* the Prince of Wales's Company, which is now the best.

I am temporarily Battalion Bombing Officer, till Gwynne Jones comes back, and this afternoon I took a party of men over to a place two miles away to do bombing tests. I left them with the Bombing Officer and returned in two hours; they were kept for another hour after that before they finished, and then I brought them back and arranged tea for them, etc.

I have been given a platoon (No. 4 of the Prince of Wales's Company), which is to be mine permanently. They are a good lot of men, but one has to be strict with them, though all the time I feel such an affection for them.

This morning we did bayonet fighting, musketry and gas drill. We parade at 10 a.m. every morning, which is a splendid hour!

A flight of five herons has just flown over the camp.

There was much amusement, and cries of "Lights out!"
They look exactly like aeroplanes!

Well, dear Mother, you know I think of you constantly. This is a most beautiful spot, and I am with
people I like, so I am as happy as I could expect to be
so far from you all. God bless you.—Your loving

CHRISTOPHER.

DEAREST MOTHER,—Your photographs just arrived. They are quite glorious and quite perfect. They
are really *you*, and it is a joy to have them. Nothing
could have given me greater pleasure, and I like the
case and everything so much. . . . God bless you.
You are continually in my thoughts.—Ever your loving

CRUFF.

I shall have your photographs with me always.

THE SALIENT [1]

The Ypres Salient[2] no longer exists. The battles of
the summer campaign of 1917 have extended the British line forward to the Passchendaele ridges and have
widened out of recognition the narrow loop of defences
that swung round to the north and south of Ypres.
But the memory of the Ypres Salient will never fade
from the minds of those who knew it in being.

[1] This description of the neighbourhood of Ypres is here reproduced by the permission of the writer, Mr. Fred Ambrose, and of the
owners of the *Welsh Outlook* in which it first appeared.
[2] A salient in a system of defences is a loop in a line of trenches
and redoubts thrust forward for a considerable distance from the
main trend of the defences.

The early battles against the westward advancing Germans barred their progress to the sea. The thin khaki line of British regulars and territorials held the beautiful old Belgian town against the most desperate attacks of the flower of the German Army, and in the varying fortunes of that period was the Salient formed —a settled integral part of the British line. The holding of the Salient was rather a matter of British honour and pride than of military importance. While it was held there was still a Belgium; still was Belgium in part free. The cost of its holding will never be told—this sector with a sinister reputation which claimed a constant heavy toll of British men. When on the Laventie stretch farther south or in the Festubert "islands" the first Kitchener's men groused about the heavy German gunfire, the old "sweats" would smile grimly, saying, "Wait till yer gets to Wypers, chum, ye'll have something to grouse about then. They shoot yer in the back as yer walks towards the line there."

And the new divisions came to regard the Salient as a Hell amongst Hells.

If you have ever visited the Fen country you will be able to picture the interior of the Salient. Low-lying, marshy, a sea of mud in winter, a few rare and scattered undulations which are a little less wet and muddy, frequent copses of stunted oaks, and fields of hop-poles—gaunt and bare in winter, but in summer clothed with wondrous green foliage; these are the characteristic features of that spit of land which was the foremost bastion of the British defences.

Round Ypres the line swept like the edge of an open fan. Where its radiating ribs met stands Poperinghe, a little town with cobbled streets and houses of quaint Flemish design with truncated gables and red-tiled roofs. Eastwards through Poperinghe passes the main road from Calais to Ypres. Half-way between Poperinghe and Ypres it runs through the village of Vlamertinghe. Elverdinghe and Woeston on the north, and Kimmel and St. Eloi on the south, flank the Salient.

Surrounding the low land held by the British, rose arrogantly the Pilkem ridge on the north, and the Messines ridge to the south—ridges upon which for nearly three years the German positions were established. They looked down upon us as into a cup-shaped hollow: they mocked us: they gave us the feeling that our every movement was being watched and all that was done was done by the tacit permission of the Germans. That hollow one entered as one would enter the Valley of the Shadow, conscious of malevolent eyes, dreading every moment evil from an invisible, ever-vigilant foe. Within the Salient to the south rose one low ridge, relieving the flat monotony, and when the air was clear on this could be discerned the old monastery of Mont des Cato, and along the edge of this ridge the canvas sails of the Flemish windmills revolved slowly in the breeze, and peacefully ground the corn into meal. In the fields toiled the peasants, on the ridge the windmills turned lazily—and from the copse near by came the full-throated roar of a big gun battery. A strange mingling of Peace and War!

Often have I lain awake under the brown blankets in my billet in the Salient, seeing the yellow glare of the Very lights, and listening to the monotonous rattle of the ration limbers returning empty from the line over the cobbled (*pavé*) roads. *The car rattling over the stony street*—Byron's line revealed then its full meaning to me. At night the guns concentrated in the hollow roared their thunder, and lit up the darkness with their lightning flashes. It seemed as though a thousand thunder-storms were concentrating their fury upon the Salient. And the ruined city—guiltless, martyred, immortal Ypres—has been exposed for three years to the fury of the storm of steel. At times an uncanny silence brooded over its pitiful streets of houses, now masses of formless debris. Now and then a gun spoke hollowly amidst its ruins making the silence more intense. Then would come the storm periods with their hissings of angry projectiles, the roar of concealed batteries, and the heart-clutching detonations of the shells that daily, and not without success, sought their mark. Then like an April shower the storm would pass, ending in a few desultory rounds from the guns, answered by stray shells whining like souls lost in the brooding silence.

Coming from the "Ramparts" near the Menin gate we traversed the ruined streets as far as the Square.

As we walked the sun shone serenely, pitilessly upon that naked heap of ruins. Through the Square flanked by the shattered Cloth Hall rode a cyclist-soldier, whistling cheerfully for he had nearly attained his journey's end. Another whistle—louder and ominous—stifled it and then a crash as a huge shell burst a little to one side of him sending up a soot-black acrid cloud of smoke. The cyclist fell headlong from his cycle and lay upon his back on the cobbled stones in the sun, his knees drawn up nearly touching his chin and his legs kicking feebly. A piece of the shell had cut across his body and had almost disembowelled him. He kicked a little more, frothed at the lips—a bloody froth—and, crouched up in that horrible attitude, lay stiff and still. And the sun shone on, warming the *pavé* stones with its rays. Everything was just the same except that lad who, but a few moments before, was whistling cheerfully, and now lay dead. The sun shone on serenely seeming to smile through death. That lad was just one of the daily toll of men who died that we might still say, "We hold Ypres."

Along the banks of the little Yperlee which flows northwards from Ypres for some distance parallel to the Yser were the dug-outs—now little needed—of the British troops who had sapped into the banks, and constructed innumerable sand-bagged shelters for themselves. Endless tracks of duck-boards stretched along its banks and that of the Yser, and here in a pre-historic fashion lived for nearly three years the troops who held the northern portion of the Salient. This dug-out town was self-contained: it had its bath, its hospital, its kitchens, its stores, its canteens, its railways, and its cemetery, in which an ever-increasing number of wooden crosses grew out of the soil, and in which there were always a number of ready-delved graves for the occupants that never failed them. And within a stone's throw there was gay laughter and song, jokes and harmless horse-play, amongst those for whom those graves yawned insatiate.

Elverdinghe—the fortress village surrounded by batteries which spoke often and seldom were wanting of their reply! The church is a broken ruin, the churchyard a chaotic mass of broken stone, plaster, glass and the bones of men long since dead. From the cellars, roofed with sandbags, peeped the bronzed faces of the garrison. They greet passers-by with a cheerful hail. "Cheero chum! Any news! When is this bloody war going to end?"

At night the Very Lights rose and fell around one in a wide curve. From the apex of the Salient near Hooge it seemed as though they surrounded one and this intensified the feeling of helplessness and impotence which possessed one during the day. These arcs of light rose and fell all through the night, while, at intervals, various coloured lights signalled to the artillery behind. It was a beautiful spectacle, but life in the Salient does not conduce to artistic appreciation.

When the moon was full, and in the dull grey dawn, enemy planes came over and dropped their burden of deadly bombs on the canvas camp and hutments built by the troops for their shelter in the cold wet weather. When the wind was "dangerous"—no rare occurrence in the Salient—the deep note of the Strombos Horn often roused us from our sleep. This heralded an enemy gas attack and the Salient was instantly a Pandemonium. Shell-case gongs were beaten, ringing lengths of steel rail hammered with metal strikers by lusty sentries, bugles were blown, and horns blared, and a little later the artillery would partially drown the inferno of noise in an attempt to smother the enemy sector from which the gas came. From the dug-outs, tents, and huts flowed a bustling, cursing stream of men obeying the call to "Stand to" with their box-respirators worn on the chest in the "Alert" position.

The soldier "on pass" into Poperinghe was rarely allowed to feel, even for an evening, that he could shake off the hateful dread of the Salient. After a long period in the line he would walk the cobbled streets and would visit the concert party and the pictures at the Divisional Cinema near the station. Rarely was the evening's enjoyment unbroken, for from the north-east would come the unmistakable hollow crack of a German long-range high velocity gun, and the scream of the 8 in. shell that burst with an appalling crash in the cobbled square. Four minutes later, and then came another—this time perhaps perilously near the crowded cinema hall and the soldier-manager would deem it prudent to dismiss the audience —an audience that trudged despondently cursing back to the camps, while panic-stricken civilians and women bearing children in their arms, hurried past them out of the town into the open country and safety.

Of such was the Salient. During the day it pulsated with toil, at the A.S.C. dumps, and at the R.E. yards refugees prepared war material for the line which prohibited the invader from the last corner of their beloved Belgium; at the numerous ammunition dumps huge and innumerable shells were loaded into lorries bound for the gun positions. New railways were being laid down, and new roads constructed for the grand advance to come. Innumerable hutments and camps sprang up amid the copses and woods of the Salient. Fritz, his path marked by a row of white puff-balls in the sky, would come to view it all, and busy workers craned their necks to see his plane flashing in the sun, and hoped that one of our airmen would attack him. An aerial fight never proved monotonous, though it was a fairly common occurrence in the Salient.

Along the roads the refugees built themselves rows of little cabins from any and every material—from hammered out petrol cans, packing cases, biscuit tins, from mud and wattle. There they lived making many honest pennies by selling eggs and chips, doughnuts, embroidered postcards, aluminium rings and such like articles to the soldiers.

And always shells, and gunfire, and the rattle of a myriad machine guns, and the constant menace of the poison gas. And often at night the thunder of a German armoured train with its leviathan guns shelling a village or our big gun positions. And always in the distance the black puff-balls of smoke from German shrapnel bursting over Ypres.

With all its dread horror the Salient will ever be hallowed ground to Britain. Her many brave sons who lie buried there have made it "for ever England's."

FRED AMBROSE.

To his Father.

August 23rd, 1917.

DEAREST DEEDOOGE,—All well here—there is not much news to tell you, but I long to hear from you. I was Picquet Officer yesterday, and had various duties to perform. I have just been censoring the men's letters.

We had German aeroplanes over here yesterday. They came right over the camp last night, and I could hear the engines distinctly, but they did not drop bombs here. They dropped them about a mile off on casualty clearing stations, and bombed some of their own wounded. I have got everything that I want out here —but would you ask Mummy to send me a "Platoon Roll Book," to keep a list of the men in my platoon. . . . We had a terrific thunderstorm last night, and it has been raining this morning. I expect to move, possibly (!) next week, but one never knows.

I spent this morning in going over the bombs belonging to the Battalion, sorting and cleaning them up generally. I am glad to have that photograph of Cadoxton—it gives me great pleasure.

God bless you. Write soon, as the men always say in their letters.—Ever your loving

CHRISTOPHER.

August 24th.

No news to-day, but just a line to say all well. We are still in the same place, and I do not yet know when we shall move. We are having a parade to-morrow of the whole Guards' Division! A French General is going to present decorations and medals. Some of our men are getting medals, and the General will probably embrace them! I played cricket yesterday. Ballard got a kick on the leg at football, and is limping a bit, but will be all right in a day or two. I have not received any cigarettes yet from the Stores. I hope you have got some of my letters by now.

God bless you, dear Mother.

Sunday, August 26th.

DEAREST MOTHER,—All well. The fountain pen has arrived, and I am very glad to have it—many thanks for it, and also the scissors. I *do* admire the magnificent way you do up the parcels in that sort of stuff we used to mount brass rubbings on![1] All your parcels have arrived safe, and I hope you got my wire about three days ago. We go to-morrow to ——[2] for some days, then the front. When we go up we shall be in the line for four days, and then come out—whenever we do go. . . .

I find my air-bed very useful out here, as we sleep

---

[1] The parcels were sewn up in unbleached calico.
[2] A farm in the neighbourhood of Elverdinghe.

on stretchers, and the air-bed makes the whole difference in comfort. I have received a cover for my steel
helmet. My periscope has come. The Entrenching
Battalion consists of men from various regiments in
the Guards Division, and Devereux is there now, but
none of us went—I do not know why. Dickens is out
here.

My Padre's real name is not Mogg but Oldham, and
he is always called "Mog" as a nickname. No one
knows why, but I suggest it is short for "Man of God"!
God bless you, dear mother; I have you continually
before my eyes, and travel to Cadoxton in spirit very
often.

I went for a ride this afternoon on the Quarter-
master's horse, and enjoyed it.

Yesterday we had a long day. Left at 11:30,
marched four miles to a flying ground. At three we
were inspected by General Anthoine, a French General,
in magnificent blue uniform. We did not get back till
six. He did *not* embrace anyone: I was disappointed!
He had a magnificent staff in bright blue, and our
Corps Commander was there.

God bless you, dear Mother.

P.S.—(Written outside the envelope.)—Un mon-
sieur qui s'appelle Pte. Ball dans le régiment ira vous
voir. Il vient de Cadoxton, et retourne là dans quel-
ques jours en vacances.

August 27th, 1917.

DEAREST MOTHER,—All well here. We moved this
morning from our last place, and came by train here, a
journey of about ten miles. Our kit we brought with

us, and it went at eight this morning. We got here about one o'clock this afternoon. It has rained incessantly all day, but I did not get wet. I have got my black top boots on!

We all travelled in cattle trucks, all the officers in one truck, and the men crowded into others. It was very interesting, as we gradually got into the area that had once been shelled—farmhouses half demolished and churches with part of the tower blown off, also many trees all looking like the "blasted Pine," [1] stripped of branches, and in some cases mere stumps left.

We marched here from the place at which we detrained along a road lined with such trees and houses —about two miles' march—and we saw German shells occasionally bursting not more than a mile or so away. We are not up in the front line nor likely to be shelled here, but it is a moderately warm place. We are surrounded by our own guns, fairly close by, and there is a tremendous bombardment going on at present— like continuous thunder. It is all very wonderful!

When we got here the men pitched their bivouacs, and we had some lunch. I am sharing a tent with the Padre and de Satgé the interpreter, both very nice and intellectual people.

My kit is all here, but it will not go further up with

---

[1] A huge tree which had been struck by lightning and stands high on the mountain side above Cadoxton. The family party often climbed up to it for the sake of the glorious view spread out beneath, and Christopher had named it from a line in one of the songs from "The Princess," which was a special favourite of his:

"... cease to move so near the Heavens, and cease
To glide a sunbeam by the blasted Pine."

me. I am in good spirits and really enjoying the great adventure. We wear our box respirators slung over our shoulders, to be ready for gas, but we are practically safe from it here, I think.

I think this is all my news. Private Ball, who is a Cadoxton man, introduced himself to me yesterday, and I had a long talk with him. He is going on leave to Cadoxton soon, and I told him to be sure to call on you, so you may expect to see him.[1]

As to the estimate that the men formed of Christopher the following words are quoted from a contemporary note made by his mother immediately after her interview with Private Ball:

"The men would have done *anything* for him, he made himself just one of them. He never made any man feel that he thought himself above him. He *was* a man *and* a soldier! He got more out of his men than others because they did it for him with willing hearts. There was no grousing in his platoon. He had a Welsh way with him, he was always so happy and smiling. They knew what he was, the men—he was one of them. Everyone thought the world of him. I have heard remarks passed after his death among the men about what he was—I know I would have given my life for him willingly."

[1] The meeting with Private Ball took place in due course when he came home on leave on September 15th. He had been in the trenches on the night of September 2nd and 3rd, and was able to give a number of small details as to the experiences of the 1st Battalion of the Welsh Guards from the day Christopher joined it.

August 28*th*, 1917.

DEAREST MOTHER.—Many thanks for your delicious long letter. There is a tremendously strong gale blowing; our tent was nearly blown away during the night! It is finer to-day, with squalls of rain. I have got my black top boots on, which keep out the rain. I wrote daily to you from the last place, so you ought to get my letters regularly. My *Daily News* is only a day late, always!

That is a delicious poem you sent me, which I will keep in my pocket-book.[1] I have also got in my pocket the little lavender bag you sent me with the fountain pen.

Re the various questions in your letter. I sleep on a stretcher raised on wood off the ground, with my air-bed, sleeping bag, and blanket. Here I have the whole valise unrolled on a stretcher and sleep on it.

My green kit bag is very useful, and I have got my web equipment, etc., and things which are too hard or too fragile to sleep on in it. We eat off tin plates and drink out of mugs, though there are a few china plates and glasses which we may occasionally get. At the last camp we had two farmhouses for having our meals in. The best one was used by Headquarters—*i.e.* C.O., Adjutant, Second in Command, etc.—with the officers of the Prince of Wales's Com-

---

[1] A poem by Christina Rossetti which ends with the following verse:

> "Heaven overarches you and me,
>   And all earth's gardens and her graves.
> Look up with me, until we see
> The day break and the shadows flee.
> What though to-night wrecks you and me,
>   If so to-morrow saves?"

pany and No. 2. In the other farm Nos. 3 and 4 Companies messed. Here we all mess together in a small corrugated shed. The men sleep in bivouacs, and we have tents, three in a tent. Bivouacs are sheets pegged down over frames (three parts and crosspiece).

We have breakfast—eggs and bacon, tea (no coffee, alas!), bread and butter and marmalade—any time from seven to nine! I had breakfast in bed this morning, and got up at 9.30, as we had to have our meals in our tents until the mess (a shed of corrugated iron) was put up. All of us have to salute the Commanding Officer the first time we see him in the day, and if he is at breakfast we walk in and salute! I like him and get on with him. He is Scotch. Then we lunch at one, when we have meat, vegetables, sweet and cheese. Tea from four to five, and dinner at eight—soup, meat, sweet and cheese, with white wine and soda to drink. We used to have coffee, too, after lunch and dinner at our last camp.

Our present camp was a field quite full of thistles when we first came. There are crops everywhere—yellow corn, wheat, and some maize. The roads are all pavé, except the very small ones, and not comfortable for marching on. The guns go on intermittently here, and there is a 12-inch one not far off which makes a tremendous bang, but they are not firing so fiercely to-day as yesterday. . . .

I am glad you got my telegram, and I will wire whenever I come out of the line. I have not heard anything more about Paris leave, but when I know for certain I will wire.

I like that extract from "Letters of a Soldier" [1] which you send me. You know all I feel, dear Mother, and I know you will be with me in all dangers and weariness that I may have to go through. What happy days we have had together—and how love has interwoven our lives! It is a great joy to look back on delicious moments we have had. I can think of many such, and they will be a memory for ever. This whole business seems often to me just a dream, from which I shall wake to find myself in my own bed at Cadoxton, and I daresay it will seem like that when it is all over.

How strange life is! We are perplexed, but not dismayed—"Heaven over-arches you and me," and I have learnt to feel that separation cannot break the bond of love nor destroy the daily intercourse which has been ours so long. The miles by which we are divided do not matter, for we are close together in the spirit, you and I. Each day that passes I *feel* that we are conversing together, with our minds, for we

[1] Extract from "Letters of a Soldier" (the writer is a young French painter): "I should like to define the form of my conviction of better things in the near future, resulting from this war. These events prepare the way to a new life: that of the United States of Europe. After the conflict those who will have completely and filially fulfilled their obligations to their country will find themselves confronted by duties yet more grave—and the realisation of things that are now impossible. Then will be the time for them to throw their efforts into the Future—they must use their energies to wipe out the trace of the shattering contact of Nations. The French Revolution, notwithstanding its mistakes, notwithstanding some backsliding in practice, some failure in construction, did none the less · establish in man's soul this fine theory of National Unity. Well! the horrors of this War lead to the Unity of Europe, to the Unity of the race. The new State will not be established without blows and strife for an indefinite time, but without doubt the door is now open towards the new horizon." (Date, November 15th, 1914.)

know that each is thinking of the other. I feel you so near to me that when I open my eyes I expect almost to see you before me. I have never felt so strongly before this nearness of you, dear Mother, to me.

Well, the path lies before me. I feel like Childe Roland, and when I have won the Dark Tower [1]— across all this waste and desolate battlefield—I shall return, please God, to the "haven where I would be." And I hope this time will soon come, when we shall meet again and rejoice together.

Give my love to all. I am well, and in a place not unpleasant. The sun is shining, and the world looks all so bright.

Give my love to all, and especially to Deedooge, whom ask to interpret βάρυ μὲν οἰστέον δ' ὅμῶς [2] from Sophocles.

God bless you again. I look forward to all the happy days we shall have together.—Ever your loving

CRUFF.

August 29*th*, 1917.

My possessions are most adequate, and I have got everything I want. Other people's things are very insufficient when compared with mine, and de Satgé, the interpreter, said to me the other day, "What a splendid kit you have got! You must have a very loving mother!"—which I said was quite true.

Hobbs will go with me into the front line, as far

---

[1] Browning's "Childe Roland." See quotation at head of this chapter, p. 229, and p. 80. But Browning quotes it from Shakespeare, *King Lear*, III. iv.

[2] Grievous indeed, yet to be endured.

as he knows, and my kit will stay behind with the transport, except just what I take up with me.

I have to-day wired to say that I am getting Paris leave September 4th. This is practically certain, and I shall be able to go unless any very unforeseen circumstance occurs. People here say it is difficult for anyone except wives to come over, but I hope you and Deedooge will manage! Most of the officers here stay at the Ritz when they go there. Paris leave has no relation at all to English leave, which you get ten days every three months, and Paris leave cannot affect that. I have got all the parcels sent, registered and otherwise. . . .

I remember the house you are taking at Langland Bay, and I like your sketch of it! You will enjoy the change and sea air. You are constantly in my thoughts, dear Mother. Farewell for the present.—Ever your loving

CRUFF.

Extracts from letters of the same date to two other members of the family:

"We are surrounded by big guns, some firing over our heads, and the first day we arrived there was a tremendous bombardment going on. 'Fritz was getting it!' as the men said. We have had German shells right over the camp, aimed, no doubt, at guns behind us, and last night I heard them singing through the air. The Adjutant found a piece of shrapnel in the camp this morning which may have been blown from 300 yards off! I am parading at 5.30 a.m. to-morrow to take a party of ninety-eight men and march to a certain town about nine miles off. I am the only officer in charge, and I leave the men at this town and then come back. I expect I shall get a lift in a motor lorry on the way back. I expect to go to the front line the day after to-morrow and be in for four days —but I do not know at all for certain. . . . We have got a tame jackdaw as a mascot, and he was brought up from our last camp in a sandbag. He is very tame, and you can pick him up.

"You would laugh if you could see me now, dressed in riding breeches and black top boots, and sitting in my tent while the wind and rain are raging outside! Well, I can tell you that I am in Flanders, and that is about all. It is all very interesting out here, which is a great thing. The batteries of guns round here are mostly 9.2, and I went and looked at them yesterday. There is a tall tree near one of them, with a ladder going up to the top, so I climbed up and had a look round. I saw very desolate country in front. Lots of trees all stripped of leaves and branches and even bark. This is a great adventure, and I am enjoying it."

August 30th, 1917.

DEAREST MOTHER,—All well. I got your letter of 27th to-day. . . .

I expect to go into the line to-morrow night.[1] I will tell you my day to-day: I rose at 4.30 a.m., breakfasted at five, paraded at 5.30, and marched my ninety-eight men to a certain town.[2] It is a quaint old place; the eastern half has been entirely demolished

---

[1] Near Langemarck.   [2] Poperinghe.

by shelling, but all the houses stand on the west side. I put my men into the train (they are returning to the Entrenching Battalion, as we are up to full strength). Then I went and had another breakfast and came back in a lorry. On returning I found the camp deserted! I went to the Orderly Room, and the clerk said the Battalion had taken refuge about 100 yards off. I noticed shells coming right over the camp and bursting a quarter of a mile west of us, so I put on my steel helmet, and joined the other officers. They told me we had had several shells of shrapnel bursting right over the camp. None of our men were touched, but the Grenadiers, who are encamped in the same field as ourselves, had one man killed and four injured by shrapnel. However, there was no more of it after I returned. I will write again to-morrow before we go off. I hope you will come to Paris, but my leave may be put off owing to our going up into the line; as it is we shall be out at the time of my leave, and you may count on my coming, but should anything occur I will wire. . . . Love to Deedooge. God bless you. All well.—Your loving

CRUFF.

August 31st, 1917.[1]

DEAREST MOTHER,—We go into the trenches to-night. I am taking Hobbs with me. Gibbs stays at Company Headquarters, coming round occasionally, and Bonsor and I take turns, one being in the line, and one at Company Headquarters. We take alternate days. Being in the line means probably a concrete

[1] Received Tuesday, September 4th, the day after his death.

blockhouse. We shall be in four days. We first cross
a river—rolling rapidly [1]—then are met by guides who
conduct us to our destination, where we relieve other
troops. As soon as we get out of the line I will if
possible wire to you. I expect I shall not come to
Paris till the 5th of September, unless I leave a day
earlier. I do not know.

My kit I am taking up is going in two sandbags by
mules to Company Headquarters. We are going to a
very quiet part of the line, I hear, which is a good
thing. I am taking my writing pad with me, so I shall
have plenty of time to write to you at length. Both
you and Deedooge will be much in my thoughts. I
do not mind going up myself, as I feel very philosophi-
cal about danger, and I have the conviction that I
shall return to you safe. God bless and keep you. Let
not your heart be troubled. I will write frequently.
Give Deedooge my love. I have not much time to
write now as we are busy getting off.—Your loving
                                        CRUFF.

· The two following letters were found upon his body
after his death in action on September 3rd.

September 1st, 1917.

DEAREST MOTHER,—I am now sitting in a dugout
in the front line; it is a concrete blockhouse and very
strong. We left our last camp yesterday evening, then
marched about two miles on the road, then turned off
on to trenchboards which led for miles past shell holes
—nothing but mud to be seen and trees stripped of

[1] The Iser. *See* Campbell's "Hohenlinden."

branches. At length we turned off again and found our own way through the mud. (We had a guide to show us the way.) They sent some shells over, but none near us during our march, and the night was dark.

We all got settled in eventually. It is an old German trench, and really faces the wrong way. It merely consists of the trench, which is broken in several places. Last night shells dropped close to us, and I got covered with mud from them several times. In the night Gibbs and I went out in front and walked about—I cannot now tell you why—but we had shells bursting round us all the time. The men are splendid, and nobody is the least bit afraid. I was up all night, and got a little sleep this morning, and a little more after tea. I have got tins of food, and Hobbs cooks for me. To-night I go back and spend twenty-four hours at Company Headquarters while Bonsor relieves me.[1] The line is really quite quiet, though one cannot move about much by day owing to German snipers.

I am a bit tired, but very satisfied with things in general, and the men are cheerful.

God bless you, dear mother. I will wire if I can when we come out.—Your loving

CRUFF.

September 2nd, 1917.

DEAREST MOTHER,—All well. I come out to-night, and Bonsor takes my place—so by the time you get this you will know I am through all right.

I got your wire last night, also your three letters.

[1] This arrangement was altered, and he remained on duty in the front line throughout Sunday, September 2nd.

I am very sorry you cannot come to Paris.[1] Isn't it shameful only wives may go? I am going with Webb,[2] which will be nice for me. I will write when I get there.

Many thanks for that little book of poems.[3] It IS a great joy having it out here. There is nothing much to do all day except sleep now and then. Well—you can think of me in Paris. It will soon be English leave, and that will be splendid!

Webb is going to stay at the Ritz, I think, where he has been before, so I expect I might go there with him. He tried to get his papa to come over, but I expect he found it is only wives who can come!

I got hit in the face by a small piece of shrapnel this morning, but it was a spent piece, and did not even cut me.

One becomes a great fatalist out here. God bless you.—Your loving

CRUFF.

A telegram from the War Office, dated September 6th, 1917, was received at Cadoxton on the evening of that day:

"Deeply regret to inform you that Sec.-Lieut. G. C. S. Tennant, 1st Welsh Guards, was killed in action September second.[4] The Army Council express their sympathy.
"Secretary, War Office."

[1] After obtaining a passport his Mother had been refused permission to proceed to Paris by the Military Permit Office, on the ground that the Regulations provided that only the wives of officers were allowed over. This specimen of official red-tape (she considers) ought surely to be done away with in the case of mothers of unmarried officers.

[2] Mr. Webb (pp. 178, 277) was killed in action on Dec. 1, 1917.

[3] A small paper-covered anthology, "The Hundred Best Poems in the English Language (Lyrical)." Selected by Adam L. Gowans, M.A.

[4] This was subsequently corrected to September 3rd.

(OF THE DEAD.)

"First and chiefly, I at least see ground to believe that their state is one of endless evolution in wisdom and in love. Their loves of earth persist; and most of all those highest loves which seek their outlet in adoration and worship. . . . For in that world love is actually self-preservation, the Communion of Saints not only adorns but constitutes the Life Everlasting. Nay, from the law of telepathy it follows that that Communion is valid for us here and now. Even now the love of souls departed makes answer to our invocations. Even now our loving memory—love is itself a prayer—supports and strengthens those delivered spirits upon their upward way. No wonder; since we are to them but as fellow-travellers shrouded in a mist; 'neither death nor life, nor height, nor depth, nor any other creature' can bar us from the hearth-fires of the universe, or hide for more than a moment the inconceivable oneness of souls." [1]

" Ἐπιόντος ἄρα θανάτου ἐπὶ τὸν ἄνθρωπον τὸ μὲν θνητόν, ὡς ἔοικεν, αὐτοῦ ἀποθνῄσκει, τὸ δ' ἀθάνατον σῶν καὶ ἀδιάφθορον οἴχεται ἀπιόν, ὑπεκχωρῆσαν τῷ θανάτῳ." [2]

A DDIODDEFODD A ORFU [3]

[1] From a Paper read before the Synthetic Society in March, 1899, by F. W. H. Myers. *See* "Human Personality," chap. x.
[2] Plato, Phædo (106): "Then when death comes to a man, his mortal part dies, but the immortal part goes away unharmed and undestroyed, withdrawing from death."
[3] "He who has suffered has conquered." The Motto of Jestyn Ap Gurgan, who ruled over Neath before the coming of the Normans.

CHAPTER XII

LETTERS FROM BROTHER OFFICERS, NON-COMMIS-
SIONED OFFICERS AND MEN OF THE WELSH
GUARDS, AND FROM FRIENDS

> "And so of all that form inheriteth
>   The fall doth pass the rise in worth;
> For birth hath in itself the germ of death,
>   But death hath in itself the germ of birth.
> It is the falling acorn buds the tree,
> The falling rain that bears the greenery,
>   The fern-plants moulder when the ferns arise.
>   For there is nothing lives but something dies,
> And there is nothing dies but something lives.
>   Till skies be fugitives,
> Till Time, the hidden root of Change, updries,
> Are Birth and Death inseparable on earth;
> For they are twain yet one, and Death is Birth."

FRANCIS THOMPSON, "Ode to the Setting Sun." (Cf. p. 108.)

FROM CAPTAIN ARTHUR GIBBS, COMMANDING THE
PRINCE OF WALES COMPANY, 1ST BATTALION
WELSH GUARDS.

1st Welsh Guards, B.E.F.
September 5th.

DEAR MRS. TENNANT,—It is with the greatest sorrow that I have to write to you about the death of your
son. I will tell you how it happened.

He had been up in the front line for two days, and

263

early in the morning of the 3rd, at about four o'clock, while it was still dark, he came down to Company Headquarters with all his kit packed up, as he was going out of the line that morning to go to Paris the next day. I saw him then, wished him good luck, and that was the last I saw of him. He had Hobbs, his servant, with him, and Lewis, an Orderly. They had only got about 200 yards away, down the duckboard track, when a shell burst very close to them, hitting your son in the eye, and about the head and face, wounding Lewis in seven or eight places, and scratching Hobbs's face. Hobbs stayed with your son, who was unconscious from the first, and Lewis, very pluckily, struggled back to Company Headquarters to fetch the stretcher-bearers. Lewis was hit in both legs, and lost a great deal of blood; he delivered his message and then fainted away.[1] Your son died in less than half an hour,[2] and I am certain he never suffered at all; I asked our medical officer specially about this. His body was brought down here, and was buried yesterday by our chaplain, the Revd. G. M. S. Oldham, at Canada Farm.

I am sending you a map of his (your son's),[3] and I have marked with a blue cross the exact spot where he was killed. It is just south of a place marked Cannes Farm, and north-east of Wijden Drift. It is on the right of the map. He is buried at Canada Farm, which I have marked with blue, which is on the left

[1] For his devotion to duty on this occasion Private J. Lewis was awarded the Military Medal. He is a Cardiganshire man.

[2] Evidence subsequently received makes it clear that death occurred within a few minutes.

[3] *Cf.* pp. 210 and 211.

of the map.   Canada Farm is about six miles north-east of Poperinghe, near the Poperinghe—Elverdinghe Road.

I am sending home in a registered parcel his small belongings which were on him.   Wrist watch, identity disc, pen, diary, flask, pipe, map, compass, cigarette case, whistle, writing pad.

Mr. Bonsor is going to make an inventory of his large kit this afternoon, and it will be sent off, c/o Cox's, who will send it on to you.   His revolvers, field glasses, periscope, etc., will be in that kit, and it ought to be home in about a fortnight or three weeks.

He had only been with us such a short time that it seems very hard that he should be killed so soon, and so young.

What work I gave him to do he always did excellently, and he was splendid up in the trenches, for his first time.   He didn't seem to care a bit about the shells. The men loved him for that.   Although he was so young they all respected him, and knew at once that he was a good officer.   I feel his loss very keenly, and can only offer you my very sincerest sympathy.—Yours very sincerely,

ARTHUR GIBBS.

Will you please write and ask me anything you want to know?

EXTRACT FROM A FURTHER LETTER FROM CAPTAIN GIBBS, DATED SEPTEMBER 14TH, 1917.

I was so glad to hear all that you had to say about your son. . . .   I am particularly happy to know that he loved the Regiment so, and that he felt so much at home with us all. It is always so strange and uncomfortable for a new officer, on joining a battalion, and one's first three or four weeks out here are always the worst.

Duckboards, or trenchboards, are short lengths of wooden track laid down in the mud, either in the open, or in the bottom of the trench, to make it possible to walk about when the country gets wet. There are miles and miles of this track laid down over the country which we have just captured from the Germans. The ground is so very much cut up by our shells that one couldn't get about without duckboards to walk upon. They are about 10 ft. long and 2 ft. wide.

Company Headquarters are usually a little way behind the front line. Last time mine were about 200 yards behind, and a duckboard track ran from Company Headquarters to Battalion Headquarters.

Your son died where he was hit. His body was taken down to Battalion Headquarters, and was carried out from there down to the canal, where it was put on a limber and taken back to our transport. . . . All the men are very upset about Christopher's death, and they still talk about him, and they miss him very much. They are always so fond of young officers, and it is very nice to see the way they look after a young boy who hasn't been out here before, helping him in a lot of small ways, especially up in the trenches.

FROM LIEUT.-COLONEL DOUGLAS GORDON, D.S.O., OFFICER COMMANDING THE 1ST BATTALION WELSH GUARDS.

1st Battalion Welsh Guards.

12.9.17.

DEAR MRS. TENNANT,—Firstly I want to tell you how very truly sorry, not only I myself am, but the whole Battalion is, in the very great loss which you have suffered, and we all grieve with you.

Your boy was only with us such a very short time, but during that period he got himself liked by all, and was so keen and took such an interest in everything. He was, too, I think very happy; he was always cheerful and smiling.

He is buried in a very nice cemetery not far from Poperinghe. His grave is at the end of the row, and he has men of the Battalion next to him. If I can do anything of any description, or tell you anything, I beg of you to ask me, and I will do all I can.

Once again please accept my sincerest sympathy, and believe me, yours sincerely,

DOUGLAS GORDON.

FROM COLONEL LORD HARLECH, WELSH GUARDS.

Regimental Headquarters, Welsh Guards, Buckingham Gate, London, S.W.1.

September 7th, 1917.

DEAR MRS. TENNANT,—It is my sad duty to write and inform you that I this morning received a letter from Colonel Gordon to say that your son had been killed as he was coming out of the trenches at dawn on the morning of the 3rd. He was hit in the head, and died without any pain.

I am afraid any words I can put to paper will fail to express my deep sympathy with you in the loss of so promising a son. The short time he had been in the Regiment was quite sufficient for his Brother Officers to find out what a valuable addition he was to the Regiment, and all who came in contact with him will grieve at his loss, but to you, I am sure, it is quite irreparable. His C.O. says that he only came across him for the first time on the 18th of last month, but the little he saw of him he liked immensely. He adds that he always seemed so happy and cheerful. We can ill spare young men like him in the Regiment.—I am, yours sincerely,

HARLECH.

EXTRACT FROM LETTER FROM CAPTAIN WILLIAMS BULKELEY,[1] REGIMENTAL ADJUTANT, WELSH GUARDS.

"I at once marked him as a really good boy, and one of the right sort. He was most popular with all who knew him, and a keen soldier, who, if time had allowed, would have made a name for himself. It is always the good ones that are taken much too soon."

---

[1] Wounded December, 1915, and awarded the Military Cross; died after a long illness consequent on wounds, March, 1918.

EXTRACT FROM LETTER FROM CAPTAIN W. A. FOX-PITT, M.C., ADJUTANT, 2ND (RESERVE) BATTALION, WELSH GUARDS.

"I knew your son very well while he was with the (Reserve) Battalion, and we all know what a loss the Regiment has suffered by his death.

"He is the sort of officer it is pleasant to have under one, and as his Adjutant I could always rely upon him to do any job he was given properly.

". . . The first thing that people noticed were his good manners, and when one got to know him one realised what a great gentleman he was and what an extraordinarily nice mind he had got; he always struck me as being very young for his age, but, on the other hand, perfectly capable to talk about any subject, and to have opinions that were his own."

LETTER FROM SEC.-LIEUT. C. PENFOLD BALLARD, WELSH GUARDS.[1]

B.E.F., France, 6.8.17.

DEAR MRS. TENNANT,—This is the first opportunity I have had, since leaving the "line" for this rest camp two days ago, of writing to express my deepest sympathy with you in the irreparable loss you have sustained in the death of your dear son. I had the warmest regard for him, and feel I have lost a true friend.

At twelve o'clock on the night before he was hit he visited my dug-out—his position was next mine—

[1] Mr. Ballard was killed in action, March 10th, 1918.

and we had a cigarette together. I then saw him to his dug-out, when he told me he was very disappointed he had received a wire saying you were prevented from going to Paris, but that he was going there alone after he had left Company Headquarters at 3.30 a.m. It was after leaving there he was struck down by a shell. I have seen his servant, Hobbs, who was also slightly wounded, and he has given me full particulars. Hobbs has looked after your son with the greatest assiduity and kindly care, and is very cut up. I was not out of the line in time to attend his funeral, but I have seen his grave, which is in a very nice position here. . . . —I remain, yours very sincerely,

CHAS. PENFOLD BALLARD.

EXTRACT FROM A FURTHER LETTER FROM SEC.-LIEUT. BALLARD, DATED SEPTEMBER 9TH.

"Your dear son and myself had always something in common. We shared the same tent before going into the line, and he showed me your photographs, which he always placed open near his bed at night. I was in command of No. 10 and half of No. 9 platoon, and the Prince of Wales's was next me, and as our dug-outs were only 15 yards apart we always visited one another once or twice a day. Your son was in my dug-out and I saw him to his at twelve o'clock, a few hours before his death, which occurred a few hours later on the duckboards. . . . He was unusually bright and cheerful—so much so that I could not help remarking it. He often told me he loved the Welsh

Guards.   I know they loved him, as I have seen letters written by the men, which I have censored."

EXTRACT FROM LETTER FROM THE REV. G. MILES
   STAVELEY OLDHAM, C.F., ATTACHED TO THE 1ST
   BATTALION WELSH GUARDS.[1]

October 4th, 1917.
   I have waited a bit to answer your letter to me about
your son until I could get a quiet time.   We were having an unpleasant time and moving about a good deal
when your letter came, which makes letter-writing difficult. . . .   I think you will like me to tell you all I
knew of Christopher.   He came to the Battalion when
we were in a very jolly camp, some miles behind the
line, and he very quickly entered into things—playing cricket with his Company, and in scratch games.
I was attracted to him at once as he was an old Wykehamist—as so many of my Oxford friends were—and
I was always brought up to venerate the old English
schools, and we had old associations with Winchester
at Westminster (where I was), and I played football
against them one year for my College.   I think everyone too liked him because he was quiet and did not
"thrust himself forward" in the mess, while at the
same time he entered into things and could obviously
hold his own in conversation and otherwise when it
came to the point.   I remember, too, his telling me
how delighted he was to find a number of men from his
own part of Wales—he was so awfully keen on his
country—and on the other side one or two men men-

[1] *See* pp. 237, 249.

tioned to me that "Mr. Tennant" came from their part, and had spoken to them of it—which they appreciated; they spoke of this to me both before and after he was killed. I recollect, too, one evening when the German aeroplanes were round about dropping bombs, and our guns were firing, that we talked about what it was like to be under fire; and I think that we came to the conclusion that it was not the fear of death, but rather the "not knowing" what being under fire would be like, and what one would find difficult, that was the worst part. When I was sharing a tent with him at the end of August I noticed that he was very fond of reading, and one night at mess we had a long talk on books. . . . and we had a great exchange of ideas and likes and dislikes on the subject; and I think we had a discussion as to whether history should not play a very much larger part in all education than it does to-day.

My last recollection of your son is seeing him in his service equipment just before he marched off to the trenches with his Company. He was quite cheery and happy, and his usual self in every way, as far as I could tell; and I think he would be.

I was up the line the day he was killed, and on my way back called in at the Regimental Aid Post to take his servant Hobbs down with our party. I noticed Hobbs was shaken a good deal by the loss of your son; his own wounds were quite slight. Hobbs, as you know, is a splendid man, and he has since talked to me of your son two or three times, and I know he was very delighted to be Christopher's servant. I shall certainly try to keep in touch with Hobbs.

Your son was buried in a military cemetery, and his grave is followed by seven of his fellow Welsh Guardsmen in the same row. Your son's is the first in the row. They have all similar crosses, just with their name and rank, regiment, and "killed in action," with the date, and a regimental badge at the top of the cross. I think it is one of the good points out here that officers and men are treated exactly alike when it comes to their last earthly incident. Christopher's body was wrapped in a blanket, covered with the Union Jack (we have not got a Red Dragon of Wales), and there was no music. Highland pipers are the only ones I have heard playing at a funeral out here. The place is well within sound and reach of shells, but I cannot be quite certain whether the guns were firing at the moment, though I have often noticed them when taking services at the same cemetery. The officers present were Major R. Luxmore-Ball, Lieut. Keith Menzies, Lieut. Francis Fripp. The Commanding Officer and all the other officers were in the line, of course, at the time, and so could not attend. I took the service, and all the men not in the line were present. . . .

I think you may care to know the exact Service which I read. I like to read always exactly the same Service for officers and men, and you will understand that the men are not all accustomed to our Prayer Book Services; and that they are not easy conditions for a Service, to stand for a long time, sometimes when shells may be near. I have tried therefore to make the Burial Service rather short, so that the men may attend carefully all the time, and as simple as possible, that they may understand it, and I have tried to bring out the glorious hope of Resurrection to Eternal Life, and the fact that the soldier's spirit—his real self— still lives, and that we are burying the body only. So I enclose the exact form of Service I read, and I ask you to forgive me if you are disappointed that the full Prayer Book Service was not used, and if the alterations and additions jar upon you. I do appreciate so much the view of those who love our Prayer Book and wish for that only; but out here I do also feel the other side. So, if I have done less than you would have liked, I can only ask you to forgive me, and to feel something of a Chaplain's difficulties out here, dealing with "all sorts and conditions of men," and yet for whom there is "One God and Father of all." —I remain, yours sincerely,

G. MILES STAVELEY OLDHAM.

THE SERVICE.

Versicles.

"I am the Resurrection, and the Life: he that believeth in Me, though he were dead, yet shall he live: and whosoever liveth and believeth in Me shall never die."

"We brought nothing into this world, and it is certain we can carry nothing out."

"The Lord gave and the Lord hath taken away; blessed be the name of the Lord."

Psalm xxiii. (in full).

The Lesson. Parts of 1 Corinthians xv., as follows.

But now is Christ risen from the dead, and become the first-fruits of them that slept. For since by man came death, by man came also the resurrection of the dead. For as in Adam all die, even so in Christ shall all be made alive. But every man in his own order; Christ the firstfruits; afterwards they that are Christ's at His coming. Then shall be brought to pass the saying that is written, Death is swallowed up in Victory. . . . O death, where is thy sting? O grave, where is thy victory? But thanks be to God, which giveth us the victory through our Lord Jesus Christ. Therefore, my beloved brethren, be ye steadfast, unmoveable, always abounding in the work of the Lord, forasmuch as ye know that your labour is not in vain in the Lord.

Committal Prayer.

As in Prayer Book, substituting "our comrade" for "our dear brother."

Versicle.

"I heard a voice from heaven, saying unto me, Write, from henceforth blessed are the dead which die in the Lord: even so saith the Spirit; for they rest from their labours."

The Lord's Prayer.

Prayer of Commendation.

"Almighty God, with whom do live the spirits of them that depart in the faith and fear of the Lord, we commend to Thy loving mercy the soul of this our comrade who has laid down his life in the service of his country. We pray Thee to pardon all his sins, and to show Thyself unto him in Thy saving grace: that so he may pass from this earthly strife into the peace and joy of Thy Heavenly Kingdom: through Jesus Christ our Lord and Saviour."

Prayer for Those who Mourn at Home.

"Almighty God, our Heavenly Father, regard with Thy tender compassion those at home to whom this our comrade is near and dear. Strengthen them to bear their sorrow, and lead them to put all their hope and trust in Thy loving mercy and Fatherly care: through Jesus Christ, our Lord and Saviour."

The Blessing.

"Unto God's gracious mercy and protection we commit thee: and the blessing of God Almighty, the Father, the Son, and the Holy Spirit, be with thee, now and for evermore." Amen.

The body is saluted by each officer as he leaves the grave-side in turn.

FROM MR. H. DE SATGÉ, ATTACHED 1ST BATTALION WELSH GUARDS.

12.9.17.

DEAR MRS. TENNANT,—Ballard told me that you would like to hear from me, or I would not, a total stranger, intrude on your great sorrow, but I should like to express my deep sympathy in your great loss. I shared a tent with your son, and had an opportunity of learning to know him and appreciate his lovable nature and many qualities. I have had in my eleven years' experience as a master at Eton College the best opportunity of studying young boys and men, and your son struck me as being one of the best products of your fine public schools. He was so keen and straight, and had such nice manners. It seems such a cruel shame that such a promising young life should have come to such a tragic and sudden end, and I can well understand what a terrible blow his death is to you. He was so proud of you, and showed me your photograph, and spoke of you as I hope my son may speak of his mother and me. Please do not take the trouble to answer this poor expression of my real sympathy and sorrow.—Yours very truly,

J. C. H. DE SATGÉ.

From Sec.-Lieut. T. H. B. Webb, Welsh Guards.[1]

Welsh Guards, B.E.F.
September 13th.

Dear Mrs. Tennant,—I feel that you may perhaps like to hear from me, as being the person who probably knew your son better than anyone else in the Regiment. I was, as you may know, at Winchester with him for four years, and came out here at the same time as he did.

I know he enjoyed his life out here and with the 2nd Battalion thoroughly. In fact, he told me out here that he was having the best time of his life. He was popular with everybody, and had the respect of his men, as he was always cheerful, and very cool under fire. He did his job excellently for the whole time he was out here.

With regard to his death, I know you have heard the whole story from his servant, Hobbs. It was quite unavoidable, just one of those bits of bad luck which go to make up this business of war. The great thing is, he was doing his job up in the line, and did not get hit by a stray shell miles behind, which is the fate of many poor people. Also he was killed practically outright and suffered nothing. If he was going to be knocked out it could not possibly have happened in a better way. But even so the whole thing is a horrible affair, and I can only express my sympathy with you, and sorrow that the Regiment has lost such a good officer. If there is anything else I could tell

[1] Mr. Webb was killed in action December 1st, 1917.

you about him, I should be only too pleased to do so.
—Yours sincerely,

T. H. B. WEBB.

B.E.F., September 24th, 1917.

DEAR MRS. TENNANT,—My last letter must have
seemed. to you to be rather formal and scrappy. This
was due to a certain diffidence I felt in pushing myself forward on such a subject, but now that you
have asked me to enter on a more intimate corre-
spondence I will gladly do so. It is the least we
who have the luck can do for those who don't; to
help to bridge the great gulf fixed between them and
their folk at home and to bring the history of their
time out here to the ears of those whom it interests
most.

As to what happens afterwards, I am not surprised
to learn what his views were. Such things are,
not unnaturally perhaps, practically never discussed
amongst us out here. Of course, such thoughts are
present in the minds of most of us, and that is the
reason we steer so very clear of them in our talk. But
to me it seems incredible that all these men have simply
been snuffed out like a candle. If leaving this world
means disappearing altogether, the whole point of stay-
ing in it disappears also, and life resolves itself into a
monstrous practical joke perpetrated on generations of
mankind.

With regard to the incident referred to by one of
our men on leave, I think the true story is as follows:
Captain Gibbs rang up Captain Devas to ask when
Christopher's leave was due, and, as it is never wise to

mention dates on the telephone within a mile of the enemy, as they can overhear, Captain Devas replied, "The day before my birthday," knowing that Captain Gibbs knew what day that was, *i.e.* the 5th of September, Christopher's leave being due on the 4th. My leave came off all right on that day, and I went there straight from the line. I was in during the days Christopher was there, but further to the left, and as communication was impossible by daylight there— everything had to go over the top, there being no communication trenches—I knew nothing about his death till the evening of that day, in fact just before I started for Paris. . . .

We were only under fire once together, and on that occasion he displayed the utmost coolness. He always said it was no good worrying, as it would make no difference to the ultimate result.—Yours sincerely,

T. H. B. WEBB.

FROM LIEUT. GEOFFREY C. H. CRAWSHAY, WELSH GUARDS [1]

*White's, St. James's Street, S.W.*1.

24.9.17.

DEAR MRS. TENNANT,—I haven't written to you before because I felt I couldn't express all that I wanted to say to you. It is so much easier to write about something which one doesn't feel too deeply.

There was something about Christopher which placed him on a level so much above those of his own age. I always thought it was mainly due to his home in-

[1] *See* pp. 211 and 223.

fluence. The love he had for you, his home, and Wales, came first in his life; and then he stood for so much that was good and best in the world.

I can but be thankful that I knew him, if even for so short a time, for I shall never forget him. To me and all those in the Regiment who knew him his name must ever be an affectionate memory. Pray God that the sacrifice of such a glorious life may not be in vain. Some day I hope to meet you, and then perhaps merely by a handshake you may know that there is one who deeply shares your sorrow.—Believe me, yours very sincerely,

GEOFFREY C. H. CRAWSHAY.

EXTRACT FROM A LETTER OF SEPTEMBER 18TH, 1917, FROM PRIVATE HOBBS, WHO ACTED AS SERVANT TO G. C. S. T. IN FRANCE AND FLANDERS.

On September 3rd, Mr. Tennant, his Orderly, and I were leaving the trenches, when suddenly they opened a barrage just where we were—we were only about one foot apart. We instantly fell to the floor, and I heard Mr. Tennant say, "Oh, Hobbs, I'm hit in the eye!"

He was a very brave Officer, and was very much liked by all the men in his platoon, and it came as a great shock to them when they heard the sad news. The orderly who was with Mr. Tennant until the day we left the front line for Company Headquarters was Private Rees, of the Prince of Wales's Company. We left him behind at the front line. At Headquarters we asked Lewis to show us the way down. We had not gone more than 200 yards from Headquarters when they opened the barrage. I have heard nothing of Lewis since he went away, and I do not know into what hospital he has gone.

Mr. Tennant was very jolly and interested whilst in the line, and the boys thought a lot of him. He would go amongst them and talk with them and also supply them with cigarettes. One could not wish to have a better Officer. Mr. Tennant usually spent most of his time in the line with myself and Mr. Ballard. Mr. Bonsor used to come over and see us occasionally, also Captain Gibbs, who used to think so much of him. I lost a good master in Mr. Tennant, and I shall never have another one like him.

EXTRACT FROM A LETTER FROM LANCE-CORPORAL G. H. LLEWELLYN,[1] No. 4 PLATOON, PRINCE OF WALES'S COMPANY, 1ST BATTALION WELSH GUARDS.

Though Mr. Tennant was with us so short a time, yet his stay was sufficiently long for us to realise what a sterling leader we had. His whole thought was for our comfort, and whatever comfort he could get under conditions out here he spared no effort to get for us. He also took great interest in our sport while out of the trenches, and proved himself no mean sportsman. We all will remember the great asset he was to us as a cricketer, and the pleasant times we spent with him in this pastime. In the name of the platoon I offer you our sincerest sympathy in your sad bereavement.

[1] Wounded December 1st, 1917. His home is in Swansea.

The following additional details are taken from an account given by PRIVATE WILLIAM REES, Welsh Guards, who was Christopher's Orderly during the days he was in the front line:

I first had speech with Mr. Tennant on the evening of Friday, August 31st, when No. 4 platoon started for the front line. When we were marching up Mr. Tennant called out for me, and said, "Come and walk ahead of the platoon with me." We therefore walked up to the front line—some nine miles—side by side. Mr. Tennant asked me if I was a Welshman, and on hearing that I came from Port Talbot [1] talk fell on Wales and home affairs. We got into the trenches after much clambering over mud and shell holes, and established ourselves in a concrete blockhouse. This had a concrete floor, the ceiling and sides being boarded; it was pitch dark, and was lighted by candles.

On entering we found the complete kit of an officer in the Scots Guards, and Mr. Tennant proceeded to inspect it. Some boxes of cigarettes, a small Bible, and a water-bottle, etc., were all there. The officer to whom they belonged had been wounded earlier in the day. After looking round Mr. Tennant said to me that he wanted to go and inspect the machine-gun posts out beyond No Man's Land. These were in charge of Corporal Llewellyn, a Swansea man, since wounded. Mr. Tennant was dressed as a private soldier, with black top boots, shrapnel helmet, and a rifle slung on his shoulders. He had both his revolvers.

We started over No Man's Land to visit the machine-gun posts. Mr. Tennant was a good soldier. He didn't know what fear was, but he was not reckless or foolhardy. In going over No Man's Land we were under a hail of shells, and had to throw ourselves into shell holes several times. A bombardment was going on, and the German snipers were awful; no one could move but he had a bullet past him. It was brilliant moonlight all the three nights Mr. Tennant was in the trenches, which made it more dangerous. We got to the Lewis-

[1] A few miles from Neath.

gun posts, and after inspecting them made our way back to the dug-out. Hobbs had by this time arrived with the kit and provisions. A green bolster-shaped kit bag belonging to Mr. Tennant was in the dug-out, and he used this as a seat. He read a good deal both from a paper-covered book [1] and a small blue book.

He also wrote some letters, and censored a number of men's letters. He received letters himself in the trenches, and told me he was so disappointed that his mother could not meet him in Paris where he was going on leave on September 4th.

He was specially loved by us men because he wasn't like some officers who go into their dug-outs and stay there, leaving the men outside. He had us all in all day long, his dug-out was full of private soldiers the whole time, many smoking, others writing letters. Our rations had not come up to begin with, and Mr. Tennant gave us out cigarettes. The men would have done more for him than for many another officer because he was so friendly with them, and he knew his job. He was a fine soldier, and they knew it.

After coming back from inspecting the outlying machine-gun posts, Captain Gibbs came in and questioned Mr. Tennant as to the position generally. Mr. Tennant said he had been out and inspected the posts. Captain Gibbs said, "We'd better go out again and make sure." Captain Gibbs, Mr. Tennant, and I then went out and again visited the machine-gun posts. This No Man's Land was strewn with dead—groups of them lying here and there. Mr. Tennant appeared quite calm and undisturbed—he was perfectly cheerful during the whole time he was in the line.

On the Sunday night, when Mr. Tennant was due to go out of the line on leave, Mr. Bonsor came into the dug-out and said to Mr. Tennant, "For God's sake, Tennant, get off quickly. There's a fearful bombardment going on, and it's going to get worse." Mr. Tennant replied, "I don't mind the shells; what I object to is the snipers."

His kit, etc., was gathered together, and he and I and Hobbs started off from the dug-out to go to Captain Gibbs's Headquarters. It took about ten minutes—over shell holes and through thick mud. Shells were falling all the time. We

---

[1] A small volume of poems. *See* p. 261.

reached Captain Gibbs's Headquarters safely. I had both my own and Mr. Tennant's rifle slung over my shoulders. Hobbs was carrying Mr. Tennant's kit.

After an interval Mr. Tennant, Hobbs, and Private Lewis started off from Company Headquarters to go to Battalion Headquarters on their way out of the line, and I remained in Captain Gibbs's dug-out. I had not done much more than take my equipment off when Lewis staggered in pouring with blood and said that an officer had been hit.

Stretcher bearers started at once, and I, feeling sure it must be Mr. Tennant, went with them. Shells were pouring over. We went along the duckboard and found Mr. Tennant's body lying in a shell hole beside it. I saw Mr. Tennant within five or six minutes of his being hit, and he was then dead, and his body lying in a shell hole as if it had fallen into it on being hit whilst he was standing on the duckboard.

This part of the line had been quite peaceful for weeks. A sergeant who was sent up to find out what sort of trenches we were going up to and what sort of time the regiment we were relieving had had, reported that it was a "cushy place," the Scots Guards having had hardly any casualties, and the place bearing the reputation of being quite quiet.

But from a short time before the Welsh Guards took it over it became an absolute hell. In all my experience of the trenches I never knew anything like those four days.[1] There was a rain of shells all over that particular place. On September 3rd (Mr. Tennant having been killed at dawn that day) we suffered severe casualties, and the regiment which relieved us had the same experience. A few days later the Germans during a raid entered the trench, and appeared to know every turn and the position of every post.

The letters which follow were written for the most part by intimate friends of Christopher's. They are included as having an interest for those in whom this

---

[1] Mr. Ballard told his wife that though he had been through the subsequent fighting at Houthulst Forest, and at Cambrai (in December, 1917), the memory of those days—August 31st to September 4th—remained as his worst experience of trench warfare.

record of his life and character have aroused feelings of sympathy.

EXTRACT FROM A LETTER FROM LADY BETTY BALFOUR.

Whittinghame, Prestonkirk, Scotland,
September 8th, 1917.

What does it all mean—and what through this torture of suffering and sacrifice is to evolve for mankind? Bill sent Ruth a sermon he heard at the front the beginning of this fourth year of war. It ended with these lines:—

> "In Flanders' fields the poppies blow,
> Between the crosses row on row
> That mark our place: and in the sky
> The larks, still bravely singing, fly
> Scarce heard amid the guns below.
> We are the dead. Short days ago
> We lived, felt dawn, saw sunset glow,
> Loved and were loved; and now we lie
> In Flanders' fields.

> "Take up our quarrel with the foe,
> To you from failing hands we throw
> The Torch—be yours to hold it high;
> If ye break faith with us who die,
> We shall not sleep, though poppies grow,
> In Flanders' fields." [1]

Christopher had no quarrel—and no foe. His ideals were not war ideals. His heroism none the less great. Every man who served with him must have been

[1] Lines written by Lt.-Col. J. McCrae, Canadian A.M.C.; first published in *Punch*. The author died in France in January, 1918.

the better for the companionship of his gentle, intellectual, utterly good spirit. The random brutality of this machine-war has set him free almost in his first fight—before he was hardened or besmirched—and before he had had to endure prolonged suffering. Like a beautiful flower he has been blown into safety. His ideals to carry on are your ideals, to which your life has long been consecrate. To break faith with him would be to live for anything short of the truest, the justest, the noblest. He was a pure and perfect knight, if ever there was one.

I do feel so intensely for his Father. If you can, tell him this from me—I know he was proud of and devoted to Christopher—Christopher the little loved boy—the school boy—the scholar—the soldier. How the young life passes before me—West Downs—Winchester—the Cambridge that ought to have been and never was—the Army nightmare—Christopher in his Guardsman's uniform, still so utterly his reflective, independent, humorous, gentle self—and now with one flame gone beyond us all, out of brutal surroundings for ever.

FROM MR. MONTAGUE RENDALL, HEAD MASTER OF WINCHESTER COLLEGE.

September 11*th*, 1917.

DEAR MRS. TENNANT,—I could hardly believe my eyes when I opened my paper this morning and found that your dear boy, whom I saw a week or two since, was no more. You know what I thought of him. His gentle, pure soul, which spoke through his eyes, and innate refinement of character attracted me from the beginning of his time here; he was a very gentle boy, in the truest sense of that good word.

Just at the end I got to know him well, and valued his trust and affection immensely. I know how nobly he took up work which his soul hated; I know that he found strength to stand fearlessly amid a shower of shells. How splendid!

But to you the loss must be beyond words: I can, with a full heart, and in no conventional terms, offer you my sympathy. May the memory of him, blameless and beautiful nineteen years, be your comfort.

Will you kindly send me a photograph for our War Memorial Volumes? I have one which he sent me for myself, and which I value far too much to part with it. —Yours in profound sympathy,

M. J. RENDALL.

FROM MR. ERNEST HARRISON, TUTOR OF TRINITY COLLEGE, CAMBRIDGE.[1]

Trinity College, Cambridge.
October 7th, 1917.

DEAR MRS. TENNANT,—Let me offer my deepest sympathy with you in your loss, of which your letter gave me the first news yesterday.

I feel the loss to the College and myself more keenly than in any other case of the kind that I can remember. Your son was clearly in love with Trinity in advance, and, for myself, I felt that he would soon have passed from acquaintance to friend. It is touching to read

[1] *See* p. 171.

your evidence of the value he attached to his member-
ship of our Society.

Could you spare me a copy of the photograph, I
wonder?

Let me quote a couplet that I wrote for a cemetery
behind the front:

> "Pro patria sociisque viros pro fœdere pacto
>   Vim passos hominum pax tenet alta Dei." [1]

—Yours sincerely,

E. HARRISON.

EXTRACT FROM LETTER FROM HUGH R. FRANCIS,
SENIOR PREFECT, KINGSGATE HOUSE, WIN-
CHESTER, 1914-1916.

I want to tell you how very much I have felt the
sad news about Christopher, although I do not expect
that you of all people need to hear that, for you knew
him as he really was far better than I ever could, although I can say that I knew and loved him as well as
any of his friends. I shall always remember him best
as he was during those last two and a half years at
Winchester, and especially the terms when we were
prefects together there. Like many at Winchester, I
did not learn to appreciate all that he was at once,
but it is not the people that we know and like the
most quickly that are always the best friends. I shall
always be sorry that I saw so little of him during his

---

[1] "For their fatherland and its allies and for a solemn covenant
these soldiers endured the outrages of men, and now are at rest in
the deep peace of God."

time at Sandhurst and in the Welsh Guards.   Not
many people of his talents and ideas would have taken
to the training and the life as he did, and loved it too,
as he really did.   Both he and I were looking forward
very much to seeing more of each other when he came
in to London in the autumn, and it was a real disappointment to me when I heard he was off so soon to
the front.

There is, in a way, a consolation that he should have
been taken out of what must be awful beyond belief,
so quickly and so gently; for if he had gone through
months of it, as some have, only to fall in the end, I
couldn't have felt he had had so happy a life as he has
had. . . .   I only hope that what I have written may
at least show you that his death is a loss, not only to
you, but in great measure a loss to me and all who knew
him."

From M. l'Abbé Marquand.[1]

Le Foyer du Soldat, Villa Jeanne d'Arc,
Avenue Godillot, Hyères (Var).

MADAME,—Bien souvent j'ai pensé au cher Christo-
phe, dont je garde le meilleur souvenir.   Je voulais
vous en demander de ses nouvelles depuis cette affreuse
guerre qui a fait tant de victimes!   Je n'osais le faire,
craignant d'apprendre un grand malheur. . . .   Votre
lettre m'apporte la certitude que je craignais de con-
naître.   Merci, madame, de m'avoir associé à votre dou-
leur de mère.   Cet enfant etait une merveille, et vous
aurait donné toujours des joies.   Il a fait son devoir

[1] *See* p. 109.

en voulant défendre son pays. Il est mort sur notre terre de France, que vous aimez, et que vous aimerez encore davantage. Nous saurons vous garder les corps de vos aimés—ces corps deviendront de précieuses réliques que nous honorerons et que nous vous rendrons quand le moment sera venu.

Esto vir! Oui, il a été un homme, et quel homme— au cœur si tendre et si viril! Je pleure avec vous, madame, ce cher enfant, et j'ai la certitude qu'il vit près de Dieu de cette vie qui donne le vrai bonheur. De là-haut il prie pour ceux qui souffrent et qui pleu- rent. Comme c'est réconfortant de croire à la com- munion des saints! Oui, la mort n'ôte pas la vie—elle ne fait que la changer! Vous me faîtes grand plaisir en me disant qu'il avait gardé mon souvenir. J'ai tou- jours sa photographie lorsqu'il tenait son lapin blanc dans les bras. J'ai gardé de vous tous un si bon sou- venir. Vous nous reviendrez, n'est pas? et n'oubliez pas que je vous reste entièrement dévoué. Je suis très occupé par mon aumônerie de tous les hôpitaux mili- taires. Je suis à la gare d'Hyères, où j'ai fait bâtir une église. Venez bientôt vous reposer près de nous.

Je prie pour ce cher enfant et pour vous, madame. La prière c'est le parfait trait d'union qui unit les âmes pour le temps et pour l'éternité.—Hommages respec- tueux, de votre tout dévoué,

ABBÉ MARQUAND.

To Christopher's father, from an old game-
keeper, a family retainer of the old school,
who was and is the close friend of the children at Cadoxton Lodge.

Aberdulais, near Neath.
September 14th, 1917.

DEAR SIR,—I am deeply touched with the contents
of your very kind letter, and I respectfully beg to say
that I feel extremely sorry for what has happened to
your dearly beloved son Christopher, and all who knew
him are surely sorry for his untimely death. But I
don't think that anyone of only casual acquaintance
can feel the deep heartfelt sorrow which those do who
knew him as well as I did. I very well remember it
was an anxious time at Cadoxton Lodge in the early
part of the day of his birth, and after he had safely
come into the world I had the great honour of being
the first male to see him after Dr. Lewis and his own
dear father.

By his Father I mean your own self. And after
the day of his birth I saw him many times as a baby
in arms and with his nurse in his little carriage. And
after he grew older, so that he could run about and
play and talk well by himself, I could find that he
strictly followed the advice of his parents. He was
fond of a little playsome joke, but always very truth-
ful, and I never knew him to do a thing that one could
consider sinful, or say anything to do harm to anyone.
I was of opinion that he was inspired with the Holy
Spirit strongly, and he seemed to be absolutely fearless.
And now I am convinced that he really was inspired by

an Holy Spirit, and the fact that a merciful Providence had ordained for him quite a painless death I take as a sure sign that his body was released from life so that his soul may ascend to a happier place than is to be found in this world. I believe it is part of our duty to take some consolation in the knowledge that the Almighty has a happier place than can be found in this world for the souls of the departed who were inspired by the Holy Spirit.

But I confess that 1 cannot help wishing that your dear son, Master Christopher, was still alive in the flesh.

I hope, sir, you will keep well, also Mrs. Tennant, and the two dear children that are left to you. Mrs. Meadows quite agrees with me in what I have said in this letter, and she tells me that she wishes to say respectfully that she very affectionately wishes you all well, as also does yours very obediently,

GEORGE MEADOWS.

FROM THE BRYNCOCH AND RHYDING FARMERS ON THE TENNANT ESTATE.

Plough and Harrow, Neath.
September 29th, 1917.

DEAR SIR,—The news of the great cloud of sorrow which has recently fallen upon your home has cast quite a gloom over this neighbourhood, where your gallant son was held in such high respect. We are conscious that mere human words fail to effectually soothe, as they fail to adequately express, the bitterness which must underlie a heavy trial such as that through which you and your good lady are now passing, but as loyal and devoted tenants upon your estate, we feel that we cannot refrain from encroaching upon the sacred domain of your silent grief and assure you how deeply we sympathise with you and your family in this keen bereavement, and how sincerely we pray that you may receive all the strengthening influence of Divine Power and be further sustained by the comforting memories of a young life whose noble surrender in the bud of promise (true to the best traditions of honourable and honoured ancestry) for King and Country will be recorded in golden characters upon the escutcheon of a God-fearing loving people.   It is not how long we live but what we put into it that tells, for one hour of glorious life's worth an age without a name.—Yours faithfully,

Daniel Bowen,
for the Bryncoch and Rhyding farmers.

The following letters from two young girls who were his closest girl friends are included as showing the impression he made upon those who shared many of his gayest play-hours.

"Of all the casualties that I have felt, Christopher's death is the hardest to believe. To me he was always so like a child that went through life as through a dream, so lovable, and creating an atmosphere so suggestive of absolute still peace, that I feel he can have had no part in the chaos that ended his life, and that he has just gently moved his still spirit elsewhere to continue that life in his own calm way. For him I cannot feel any tragedy, he seemed to be so cheerfully happy in any place, yet having no passionate clinging to this life. You must have been his greatest tie, and surely he, at least, will not feel that is broken. . . . I know that I shall feel him more acutely here than I ever did; so many things will remind us of Christopher that at times he will seem with us, just the same, with a hand ready and willing to help at every turn."

"I am not going to attempt to offer sympathy, it does not help; in fact I always feel it makes things *harder* to bear, except from a very few people.

I am very miserable, but chiefly for you; I always felt that dear Christopher himself was not quite of this world.

The part of him which talked, moved, and even thought, was here; but I felt that his true self was always far away, in quite another world. I never felt that he was in any way made for this existence, he was so totally unlike anyone else I ever met.

I feel, therefore, that his real self is still just where it always was, because it never was here, and that, on account of that, it is in a way less of a separation than it would be with many boys, who have their whole being essentially on this earth.

Another thing I feel is that he was a boy who had such a calm philosophy about life that it must have been easier for him to go than many boys. He himself, I mean, would not have dreaded it, for I feel he knew it would make so little difference, really.

I am sure he is happy. It is the first thing I felt very strongly after taking in what it meant. It was such a shock because it had never occurred to me as possible. I am sure that the only thing that would make him sad is your sorrow.

I am sure that the one thing he would wish would be for you not to be too unhappy. He was a great friend, and I too shall miss him dreadfully."

> "Bydd myrdd o ryfeddodau
> Ar doriad boreu wawr,
> Pan ddelo plant y tonau
> Yn iach o'r cystudd mawr;
> Oll yn eu gynau gwynion,
> Ac ar eu newydd wedd,
> Yn debyg idd eu Harglwydd,
> Yn d'od i'r làn o'r bedd."

"For he who hath thus far had intelligence of love, and hath beheld all fair things in order and aright,—he, drawing near to the end of things lovable, shall behold a BEING marvellously fair; for whose sake in truth it is that all the previous labours have been undergone: One who is from everlasting, and neither is born nor perisheth, nor can wax nor wane, nor hath change or turning or alteration of foul and fair; nor can that beauty be imagined after the fashion of face or hands or bodily parts and members, nor in any form of speech or knowledge, nor as dwelling in aught but in itself; neither in beast nor man, nor earth nor heaven, nor any other creature; but Beauty only and alone, and separate and eternal, which, albeit all other fair things partake thereof and grow and perish, itself without change or increase or diminution endures for everlasting. And whoso being led on and upward by human loves begins to see that Beauty, he is not far, I say, from reaching the end of all."—PLATO, "Symposium."

NOTES ON A FEW QUOTATIONS
AND ALLUSIONS

Most of the sources of quotation are sufficiently indicated in the body of the book; but, in case it is convenient to any reader, some residual information is unobtrusively collected here :—

Dear Land of my Fathers, whose glories were told
By bard and by minstrel who loved thee of old,
Dear country whose sires, that their sons might be free,
Have suffered and perished for thee!

Wales! Wales! Land of the mist and the wild,
Wherever I roam, though far from my home,
The Mother is calling her child.

PAGE

225. "Since in that hour" . F. W. H. Myers, "Fragments of Prose and Poetry," p. 148.

254. "Heaven overarches" . Christina Rossetti (see p. 252).

262. "Neither death nor life" Romans viii. 38.

295. Welsh poem

> There will be myriad wonders
>   At break of morning dawn,
> When the children of the tempest come
>   Freed from their great tribulation;
> All in their robes resplendent
>   And with countenance transfigured
> Resembling their Lord
>   Rising from the tomb.

Of the Dante passages, on page 204, the translation in *The Temple Classics* will serve:—

"This mountain is such, that ever at the beginning below 'tis toilsome, and the more a man ascends the less it wearies.

"Therefore when it shall seem to thee so pleasant that the ascending becomes to thee easy, even as in a boat to descend with the stream,

"Then shalt thou be at the end of this path: there hope to rest thy weariness."

. . . . .

"Thou art so nigh to the supreme weal that thou shouldst have thine eyes clear and keen."

CPSIA information can be obtained at www.ICGtesting.com
Printed in the USA
LVOW10s0557141013

356774LV00013B/169/P